THE GREAT WAR
AND THE AMERICAN
EXPERIENCE

This book was published with support from the French Ministère de la Défense,
Secrétariat Général pour l'Administration,
Direction de la Mémoire, du Patrimoine et des Archives.

Dépôt légal: March 2017
ISBN : 978-2-07-270640-0

THE GREAT WAR AND THE AMERICAN EXPERIENCE

Bruno Cabanes

Gallimard | Ministère de la Défense

14

28

48

62

96

110

124

CONTENTS

AMERICA'S FORGOTTEN WAR

Overshadowed by the epic story of soldiers in World War II, buried under the painful memory of the Vietnam, Iraq, and Afghanistan wars, World War I as experienced by American soldiers and citizens remains a little-known saga. Admittedly, the United States entered the conflict late, after choosing to remain neutral in the summer of 1914. For three years, the country was split between interventionists and isolationists. The sinking of the *Lusitania*, the submarine warfare conducted by Germany, and the Zimmermann telegram raising the threat of an alliance between the German government and Mexico were all contributing factors that pushed America into war, from its position of benevolent neutrality toward the Allies.[1] In the spring of 1917, Woodrow Wilson, the reticent president who won re-election by a tight margin in November 1916 on the slogan "He kept us out of war," mobilized an equally reticent nation. American infantrymen, known as doughboys (or Sammies, as the French called them), first saw action only one year later, in the spring of 1918. In the ensuing six months, America lost more soldiers on the European battlefields—over 53,400 men in all—than during the three years of the Korean War and the nine years of the Vietnam War. In the United States, the Great War is virtually a forgotten war. Yet it marks a turning point in the country's military history, in American society, and more broadly, in America's relationship with the rest of the world.

This book recounts the history of Americans at war through photographs in the collections of the l'Établissement de Communication et de Production Audiovisuelle de la Défense (ECPAD, Communication and Audiovisual Production Company for the Department of Defense) and in American archives. The French and American photographers provide complementary visions. For French reporters in the Section Photographique de l'Armée, created in 1915, photographs were primarily intended to illustrate the scope of the American war effort and the strength of the bonds linking the two countries. The stories depict all the events surrounding the landing of American troops in Europe. As if to contrast them with the weary bodies of the French soldiers, the images radiate the unmistakable youth of the doughboys. The Americans entering the war meant regeneration, power, and exoticism, notably illustrated by the many portraits of black soldiers. American photographers, in contrast, portrayed the advent of a modern Army, which somewhat embodied the national identity—perhaps with the goal of mitigating the perception of inexperience and improvisation noted by many European military observers.

A conscript Army The U.S. Army in the spring of 1917 was a far cry from that of World War II. There were no more than 127,500 men, along with the 181,000 members of the National Guard, half of whom were stationed along the Mexican border. The armed forces were deployed in the Philippines, Hawaii, Puerto Rico, and Alaska.

A large, powerful Army was needed in response to a world war that was being fought primarily on the European continent. On May 18, 1917, Congress

1 Michael S. Neiberg, *The Path to War. How the First World War Created Modern America*, Oxford and New York, Oxford University Press, 2016.

adopted the Selective Service Act, which allowed President Wilson to create a conscript Army. This was the first time since the Civil War that the United States had to resort to a draft, despite the population's reservations to reinstating it.

Ten million men, aged twenty-one to thirty-one, were registered by the local draft boards. This figure rose to over 24 million by August 1918, when men over eighteen and under forty-five were also registered. The Wilson administration organized a propaganda campaign promoting duty, moral obligation, and responsibility; and drew on the incentive power of "communities" (clubs, churches, schools, and so on) to build its Army of citizen soldiers.[2] "On Which Side of the Window are You?" challenged a recruiting poster, alongside an image of an elegantly dressed young man watching soldiers in uniform marching down the street. Draftees could be exempted from serving in the Army for various reasons: religious (the Quakers and the Amish, for example), professional, and above all, family (married men with dependents to support were systematically exempted). Furthermore, one in three conscripts received an exemption for physical reasons. Finally, one in four Americans was illiterate: the U.S. Army consequently developed a system of intelligence and achievement tests for each draftee, and improved the basic training program within regiments. A total of 6.3 million men were declared fit for service. Just 2.8 million would serve in active duty, alongside the regular Army, the National Guard, and volunteers, for a total of 4.8 million Americans in the armed forces.

America's mobilization was not only a military one; it was also economic and cultural. In a country that was openly hostile to excessive government involvement in the lives of private citizens, the federal authorities had to take on a new role, that of running a wartime economy. In July 1917, the War Industries Board, chaired by financier Bernard M. Baruch, was created to oversee the production of war supplies, determine prices, and standardize products. In the spring of 1918, the National War Labor Board was formed to mediate disputes between labor and management to ensure maximum productivity in war industries. Concerning national security, Congress adopted the Espionage Act on June 15, 1917, under which charges could be brought against any person suspected of conveying confidential information about the armed forces or defending the interests of the enemy. This act was expanded the following year by an amendment, the Sedition Act, which prohibited "any disloyal, profane, scurrilous, or abusive language about the form of government of the United States . . . or the flag of the United States, or the uniform of the Army or Navy." The wartime legislation was clearly contrary to the freedom of speech enshrined in the Constitution. Yet both laws, still valid under American legislation, have been upheld several times by the U.S. Supreme Court, most notably after Eugene V. Debs, who ran as a Socialist candidate for president several times, was sentenced to a ten-year prison term for his antiwar statements. Overall, on the domestic front, the mobilization in the spring of 1917 led to a dramatic increase in the power of the federal government at the expense of individual freedom.

Heading to France   On the military front, however, America's entry into the war did not alter the strategic balance among the Allies and Central Powers, at least initially. In April 1917, the U.S. Army did not have any infrastructure that could support a major international involvement or send troops to the Western Front. Thousands of men crossed the country by train to reach their training camps, and then to the ports of embarkation for Europe: Hoboken in New Jersey, and Hampton Roads in Virginia. The railways were often old and there were not enough trains. Next came the Atlantic crossing, which was especially problematic, as

2 Christopher Capozzola, *Uncle Sam Wants You. World War I and the Making of the Modern American Citizen*, Oxford and New York, Oxford University Press, 2008.

the United States did not have a fleet large enough to transport the troops. German ships, blocked on the East Coast ports since 1914, were immediately requisitioned by American authorities.

It is hard to imagine what this journey to Europe must have been like for all these men, most of whom had never even seen the ocean, as they watched the American coastline recede, discovered the high seas, and suffered from seasickness. Escorted by destroyers, the American ships always traveled in convoys. The only ship lost was the British steamship *Tuscania*, on February 5, 1918; two hundred Americans lost their lives when the ship was sunk. There was an ever-present fear of submarine attack, and sailors constantly scanned the sea with binoculars. To avoid detection by the enemy, all lights were turned off at dusk. The soldiers lived in complete darkness from nightfall to dawn. During the fifteen-day ocean crossing, boredom, lack of information, and close living conditions heightened tension among the crew. The luckiest soldiers were aboard German cruise ships seized by the Americans, like the *Vaterland*; others traveled on cargo ships that were most commonly used to transport goods and livestock.[3]

A diverse U.S. Army When the men reached the ports of Brest or Saint-Nazaire—or Le Havre for those who transited via Liverpool—they were exhausted and nearly relieved to finally set foot in Europe. It still took several months to train them in trench warfare and the use of firearms. The U.S. Army built massive camps that impressed the French civilian population. To feed the soldiers, the Army imported tons of beef that were then shipped in refrigerated wagons to the front lines. It built railways, telegraph lines, and roads. During the Civil War, combat troops formed 90 percent of the Army, while they accounted for only 40 percent during the Great War; the remainder consisted of soldiers working on logistics operations such as transport, supplies, and maintenance. In 1917 and 1918, most men of color were assigned to these logistics and supply jobs.[4]

In the eyes of a nation deeply marked by racial discrimination, African Americans remained second-class soldiers, barely combatants. Viewed as incompetent, untrustworthy, and potentially dangerous, they served in segregated units and trained in separate camps. Indeed, the decision to extend the draft to the black population triggered heated debate. Arming African Americans ran the risk of a civil war, wrote an outraged James K. Vardaman, a senator from Mississippi, known for his positions in favor of white supremacism. Race riots, which broke out near Houston in August 1917, fueled the controversy further: the rioters were court-martialed, and nineteen black soldiers were executed by hanging. Yet discrimination within the U.S. Army did not dissuade young black Americans from enlisting, in the hope that their contribution to the war effort would result in better living conditions down the line.[5]

It's hard to explain the reasons that motivated the rest of the soldiers to join the battle.[6] Some of the conscripts may have remembered German atrocities perpetuated against Belgian and French civilians during the summer of 1914. "Remember Belgium" stated one recruiting poster, while another, depicting the enemy as a gorilla wearing a pickelhaube helmet, encouraged young Americans to "Destroy this mad brute. Enlist!" Yet how many soldiers were truly receptive to the idealistic message broadcast by their country: a war for freedom and justice, and not a war of revenge and conquest? In one of his short stories, F. Scott Fitzgerald described these regiments as "country boys dying in Argonne for a phrase that was empty before their bodies withered."[7] The average age of the draftees was fairly young. Five hundred thousand of them were first-generation immigrants, half of whom did not speak English. According to

3 David R. Woodward, *The American Army and the First World War*, Cambridge, Cambridge University Press, 2014, chapter 10. **4** Jennifer D. Keene, *Doughboys, the Great War and the Remaking of America*, Baltimore and London, The Johns Hopkins University Press, 2001, p. 39. **5** Arthur E. Barbeau and Florette Henri, *The Unknown Soldiers: African American Troops in World War I*, Philadelphia: Temple University Press, 1974; Chad L. Williams, *Torchbearers of Democracy: African American Soldiers in the World War I Era*, Chapel Hill, N.C., The University of North Carolina Press, 2013. **6** Edward Gutiérrez, *Doughboys on the Great War: How American Soldiers Viewed Their Military Experience*, Lawrence, University Press of Kansas, 2014. **7** F. Scott Fitzgerald, *The Short Stories of F. Scott Fitzgerald: A New Collection*, Matthew J. Bruccoli, New York, Scribner, 1995, p. 512.

estimates, forty-six different languages were spoken by men in the U.S. Army in 1917, a situation that clearly presented an obstacle to military training. Military authorities were particularly suspicious of German- and Austrian-born conscripts: this was the largest population group to have emigrated to the United States in the early twentieth century (2.5 million people).

A fear of spies and internal enemies was widespread in the United States as early as the summer of 1914, resulting in arrests, a ban on teaching German in schools, and various forms of local discrimination, notably in the Midwest. In the spring of 1917, President Wilson introduced a new act targeting all men of German origin over the age of fourteen, defined as "enemy aliens." This act, expanded to include Austro-Hungarians in December of 1917 and women of German origin in April of 1918, required compulsory registration with the closest police station or postmaster. In addition, firearms and telegraphs were confiscated, and these individuals were banned from getting any closer than a half-mile to military installations.[8]

Fighting the war Given the cultural and ethnic diversity of its soldiers and the inexperience of its officers, the U.S. Army required several months before it could become truly operational. When the Germans launched their final major offensive on the Western Front, in March 1918, known as the Michael Offensive, there were barely more than 300,000 American soldiers in France. On March 15, 1918, nearly one year after declaring war, the War Department drew up a list of American losses: 1,212 dead, including 136 killed in combat; 134 in accidents; the rest from illness. This figure is extremely low compared to British Army casualties, which numbered 790,000 soldiers between January and November 1917.

The United States had insisted that its troops be placed exclusively under American command, and not formally incorporated into the Allied Armies. For the U.S. military, maintaining an independent command structure was an issue of national pride. But the goal was also political and diplomatic. By giving the United States the means to prove its effectiveness on the Western Front, President Wilson wanted to have considerable input when the time came for postwar discussions on reorganizing international relations. After all, the United States entered the conflict in the name of these principles, as stated by Wilson in a speech to Congress on April 2, 1917: "We have no selfish ends to serve. We desire no conquest, no dominion. We seek no indemnities for ourselves, no material compensation for the sacrifices we shall freely make. We are but one of the champions of the rights of mankind. We shall be satisfied when those rights have been made as secure as the faith and the freedom of nations can make them."

General Pershing therefore took command of the American Expeditionary Forces (AEF), and with it, the responsibility for overseeing the entire military campaign, including basic training for soldiers, troop transport to the theater of operations, and strategy on the front lines under American leadership. President Wilson and his cabinet would continue to determine the country's major political and diplomatic policies. But Pershing had a degree of latitude in relation to civil authorities that was unprecedented in the military history of the United States. He insisted that American forces be sent to combat gradually, after they had received intense training, to avoid unnecessary losses. Furthermore, he believed that his men would only achieve their maximum efficiency by 1919 or 1920. For him, as for many other Allied generals, there was no doubt at the time that the war would be a long one. The first American battles took place in Seicheprey on April 20,

8 Jörg Nagler, *Nationale Minoritäten im Krieg. "Feindliche Ausländer" und die amerikanische Heimatfront während des Ersten Weltkriegs*, Hamburg , Hamburger Edition, 2000.

1

2

3

World War I was also a war of words and images. In the United States, the Committee on Public Information worked with the most talented illustrators to produce 20 million posters, more than all the other countries at war combined, in less than two years' time. The visual propaganda sometimes depicted the theme of German atrocities (1 and 2) to encourage draftees or to promote war bond purchases. With an image of a young man hesitating to enlist (3), it appealed to other motivating emotions, like masculine pride.

1918, and in Cantigny in late May; George C. Marshall, future Chief of Staff of the United States Army during World War II, had planned the victorious Cantigny operation.[9] One month later, Belleau Wood (Aisne *département*) was the site of one of the most important battles in the history of the Marine Corps. The price of this baptism of fire was high: the 2nd Infantry Division lost 7,800 men, who were killed, wounded, or went missing in action.

During the summer of 1918, Supreme Commander of the Allied Armies Ferdinand Foch developed a two-phase plan: an initial series of limited attacks intended to reduce the salient held by the enemy, followed by a general offensive, expected to conclude in early 1919. In September, efforts by the Americans, notably the 2nd Infantry Division, targeted the Saint-Mihiel salient in Lorraine, a German-held position that had been strongly fortified since late 1914. The United States launched their forces against the enemy just as they were making a strategic retreat to a better defended position. With the support of aircraft commanded by General Billy Mitchell, the U.S. Army achieved a major victory at Saint-Mihiel, although it did not manage to gloss over the weaknesses of his command nor the logistical problems. The Army also suffered from poor coordination between the infantry and the artillery, and from training that was poorly adapted to the realities on the battlefield toward the end of the Great War.

In late September, Pershing had to rush to transfer troops to the Meuse-Argonne sector, where Marshall Foch had asked him to lead the offensive,[10] but most of his available soldiers were inexperienced, as the best had been deployed during the battle for Saint-Mihiel. The Americans initially faced five severely weakened German divisions, but were soon in serious trouble as German reinforcements poured in. The U.S. First Army lost 45,000 men, who were killed or wounded, during the first four days of the Meuse-Argonne Offensive. In all, the months of September and October, 1918, were the deadliest in terms of deaths and injuries in all American military history, even taking into account the monthly losses suffered during the Civil War and World War II.[11] Added to battle casualties was the devastation caused by the Spanish flu. From September 1 to November 18, 1918, as many soldiers died from the illness, which they developed in the United States and in Europe, as from battlefield injuries.

In early November, American forces were divided into two separate armies. Coordination between the artillery and the infantry was improved. Pershing continued to plan for a vast offensive by the Second Army toward Metz, which should have taken place by late 1918. The Armistice on November 11, 1918, put an end to his plans. In all, over 53,400 American soldiers were killed in action in World War I. This may seem a small number compared to the enormous losses suffered by the other countries at war since 1914. Yet the magnitude of the loss of human lives becomes clear with the realization that the U.S. Army only joined the battlefields in the spring of 1918, and fought for just six months. On average, during the summer and fall of 1918, the U.S. Army lost 820 soldiers per day, only slightly fewer than the 900 French soldiers who died every day.

Postwar transition Did the United States play a major role in the final victory of the Allied Forces? From a moral and psychological standpoint, it is irrefutable. But from a strictly military perspective, the answer is less clear-cut. The country's influence in the peace-building process, however, was significant. For the Americans, the goal of the Paris Peace Conference was not so much to punish Germany and the Austro-Hungarian Empire, held to be responsible for the

9 George C. Marshall, *Memoirs of my Services in the World War, 1917-1918*, Boston, Mass., Houghton Mifflin, 1976. **10** Edward G. Lengel, *To Conquer Hell: the Meuse-Argonne, 1918. The Epic Battle that Ended the First World War*, New York, Henry Holt and Co., 2008. **11** Jennifer D. Keene, *World War I. The American Soldier Experience*, Lincoln, University of Nebraska Press, 2011, pp. 19-20.

outbreak of the war, as set forth eloquently in Article 231 of the Treaty of Versailles, as to implement the ideas proposed by President Wilson in his famous Fourteen Points speech of January 8, 1918. Given this context, the American president's visit to France, which was widely covered in photographic reports, raised hopes higher than any other head of a foreign country had to this point. For several months, a period described by the historian Erez Manela as the "Wilsonian moment," nearly anything seemed possible.[12] Letters sent to Wilson by ordinary French citizens illustrate the near fervor surrounding the American president at the time.[13]

Yet for the soldiers, a yearning to return home quickly prevailed over all other issues. In contrast to their French and British allies, the Americans did not have any demobilization plan in place. No one expected the conflict to end by late 1918. The Army had to improvise. In their letters, doughboys complained of the ingratitude of French civilians, the threat of the Spanish flu, uncertainty as to their future. Would they be sent to Russia or Germany, or would they stay in France to help with reconstruction? Given the slow-moving military administration, the families of soldiers launched a campaign that was soon picked up by Congress: "Bring the boys home!" By the month of March 1919, the U.S. Navy was bringing nearly 300,000 men home every month, where they disembarked in the ports of Hoboken, New Jersey, or Newport News in Virginia. The civilian population greeted them with parades and ceremonies, widely captured in official photographs that showcased public enthusiasm and the joy of family reunions.

The general atmosphere in postwar America, however, was tinged with anxiety: a fear of the spread of Communism and racial tension, increasing unemployment, and declining social status. All the stereotypes seen in American movies from the late 1940s or after the end of the Vietnam War—those of marginalized, brutal, and spurned veterans—had already appeared in films from the 1920s. Even though the psychic trauma of war had not yet been recognized as it would be several years later, the figure of the soldier suffering from shell shock, a form of post-traumatic stress, appeared fairly regularly in postwar cinema. In 1926, with *The Stolen Ranch*, for example, William Wyler directed a psychological study of veterans, which prefigured his major post-World War II film, *The Best Years of Our Lives* (1946).

The photographs reproduced here tell a different story. Reflecting the approach of French and American reporters, they celebrate the mutual discovery of the two allied countries. They depict a dual history, that of the United States in the process of becoming a world leader, and that of France as the arrival point for an immense circulation of men and raw materials from around the globe. The Great War inaugurated the era of global conflicts. It is this fundamental shift in modern warfare that this book captures.

12 Erez Manela, *The Wilsonian Moment. Self-Determination and the International Origins of Anticolonial Nationalism*, Oxford et New York, Oxford University Press, 2007.
13 Carl Bouchard, *Cher Monsieur le Président. Quand les Français écrivaient à Woodrow Wilson (1918-1919)*, Paris, Champ Vallon, 2015.

I WANT YOU FOR THE U.S. ARMY!

In the summer of 1914, the United States decided to remain neutral in the conflict that had broken out in Europe and immediately expanded throughout the colonial empires. The decision to remain out of the war, widely debated by American politicians, can be explained by the collective belief that the war would be a short one—but also by the number of first- and second-generation immigrants living in America, who had come from both the Allied countries and those of the Central Powers. This neutrality, however, was short-lived. On an economic and financial level, it was impossible for the United States to cut itself off from the European market, which at the time was its primary importer. In 1915, President Wilson authorized short-term bank loans and trade with the warring parties. In theory, the business community could trade with all the countries, indiscriminately. But with the Allied blockade set up against the Central Powers, then the submarine war launched by the Germans, trade between the United States and Germany plummeted to just 1 percent of 1914 levels. Conversely, certain influential figures, such as the directors of the Morgan Bank, played a decisive role in consolidating the economic and financial links between the United States and Great Britain.

From a military standpoint, the United States was not ready to deploy in Europe. Yet certain politicians, like Republican senator Henry Cabot Lodge from Massachusetts and former American president Theodore Roosevelt, had called for strengthening the U.S. Army and for joining the war alongside the Allies. Roosevelt, who was fifty-five in the summer of 1914, was a war hero from the Spanish-American War of 1898. He regularly sent letters to the White House requesting authorization to take command of a division of volunteers on the Western Front. For most Americans at the time, however, the more imminent danger seemed to come from neighboring Mexico, as they feared it wanted to expand its territory to Texas, New Mexico, and Arizona—a fear confirmed in early 1917 with the episode of the Zimmermann telegram. Some 90,000 members of the National Guard were therefore stationed along the Mexican border. The regular Army

James Montgomery Flagg posing next to his famous recruitment poster in the spring of 1917. With more than 5 million copies printed, it pictured America as a severe-looking old man talking to America's youth as if to his own children. The gesture of a finger pointing at the reader was inspired by a 1914 British poster. The origins of the figure of Uncle Sam, however, remain unclear and seem to date from the early nineteenth century.

1

1
Yale Daily News staff members pose in their uniforms as young recruits. More than two hundred Yale University students, including many volunteers, lost their lives during the Great War. The names are inscribed on the walls of Woolsey Hall.

2-3
Each recruit had to undergo a medical exam. Fitness for military service was determined according to weight, height (at least 4 feet, 11 inches), and chest girth. Civilian experts viewed the creation of a draft Army as an opportunity to experiment with assessment methods. Proposed by Robert M. Yerkes, president of the American Psychological Association, tests were introduced in training camps to determine the conscripts' "intellectual quotient," a new concept at the time. These tests were derived from a theory of hereditary intelligence, influenced by racial suppositions and eugenics. Ultimately, half of the recruits would be tested during the conflict. In this photo (3), a black soldier is tested using a set of cubes.

had no more than 127,500 men—barely larger than the Belgian Army in 1914. This small contingent of soldiers, most of whom were poorly trained, was insufficient to join in a world war.

After the declaration of war in April 1917, the American government had several options for creating the Army it needed: call for volunteers, as it had done regularly in the past; institute a draft; or wait for the flow of volunteers to naturally dwindle down before setting up a conscript Army, if necessary. Concerned that the volunteer option could disrupt the national economy, the government instead opted for a conscript Army by creating the Selective Service System. In the United Kingdom during the summer of 1914, a famous recruitment poster portrayed Lord Kitchener, Secretary of State for War, pointing his finger at British youth, with the caption: "Your country needs you." Three years later, in 1917, the American illustrator James Montgomery Flagg used it as inspiration for a similar poster: "I Want YOU for U.S. Army." The familiar face of Uncle Sam, who embodied the family values of the American nation, presented a stern request for young men to participate in the war effort, a message that historian Christopher Capozzola described with the paradoxical phrase "coercive volunteerism."[1]

In other words, the American government did not make federal agents responsible for organizing the draft—to avoid a recurrence of the conflicts that marked the final two years of the Civil War. It was out of the question, for example, to send Army representatives to the homes of draftees, an invasion of privacy that many Americans found intolerable. In 1917, many of them even opposed the very idea of compulsory military service: democrats, isolationists, and labor union members feared that a powerful Army would serve the imperialist interests of the business world outside the country or be used to break strikes domestically.[2] Instead, families, schools, churches, and all the communities forming the country's social fabric were charged with promoting mobilization, by appealing to each citizen's sense of responsibility. The draftees were to show up and register at their draft boards on a certain date. The provision by which people could purchase a replacement was also eliminated.

Married men with families to support represented nearly half of the citizens who were exempt from the draft, at least temporarily. To receive an exemption, however, they had to fill out a twelve-page questionnaire, which was a deterrent to many recent immigrants who had not mastered English. Participation in an economic activity crucial to the war effort was another reason for exemption. But how to distinguish those who were actually essential to the war economy from those workers who could be mobilized? This is where the 4,647 draft boards, consisting of local representatives, came in. In southern states, large landowners used their influence to keep their labor force from being conscripted. Owners of smaller, independent farms, lacking representatives on the boards, found themselves in more precarious situations. Exemptions for industrial workers became more widespread throughout 1918, with the expanding war industry. Finally, the Selective Service Act recognized the principle of exemptions for religious reasons. The best-known conscientious objector was Sergeant Alvin C. York from Tennessee, celebrated later by Hollywood in a successful film that was released in 1941, several weeks before the Japanese attack on Pearl Harbor. In November 1917, convinced of the morality of joining the war, York finally enlisted, as did 80 percent of the other conscientious objectors at the time; he would become the most highly decorated soldier in the Great War.

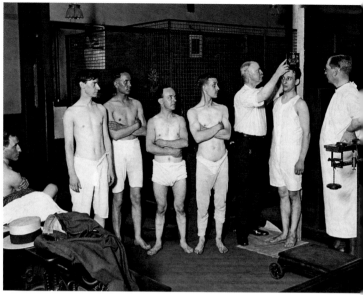

2

After receiving confirmation of their draft status, men still had to undergo a medical examination. The archives of the U.S. Army's medical department offer a remarkable overview of the country's state of health in 1917 and 1918. Approximately one-third of draftees were exempted for physical reasons, notably those who lived in the industrial areas of the northeast United States. Men with heart conditions, epilepsy, or tuberculosis, for example, were systematically declared unfit to serve in the armed services. In the end, men from rural environments and from the urban middle and upper classes, who were either healthier or at lower risk of illness than laborers, were over-represented in the armed forces.

In the summer of 1917, the first group of conscripts boarded trains taking them to their training camps, while in France, the Regular Army had already been landing its first contingents since the month of June. Men left their homes laden with provisions from their families, including homemade cookies and bottles of alcohol. The train cars were covered with anti-German graffiti, draped in red, white, and blue flags, and decorated with branches. When they finally reached the military camps, in their own clothes and wearing their soft-brimmed hats or caps, the draftees still looked like civilians, and knew nothing about warfare. The brochure *Home Reading Course for Citizen-Soldiers*, which they received in the mail before leaving, did little to offer them a realistic view of warfare on the Western Front. The Army recommended that they prepare for war as if it were an athletic competition, with daily exercise, no smoking, a good night's sleep, and no sweet drinks ("keep away from soda fountains and soft-drink stands). The

3

1

new reality of total warfare was sugar-coated: "There is probably little basis for the idea that the number of casualties in this war is any greater, in proportion to the number of men engaged, than in previous wars. In the French Army during the last six months of 1914 (which included three major offensives), the total losses with respect to those killed, wounded, or taken prisoner are officially reported to have been only 1.28 percent of the French forces under arms."[3]

The first days in the camp involved an introduction to military discipline, tetanus and typhoid vaccinations, psychological testing—introduced for the first time in 1917—and physical exercise. Training primarily involved drills, and learning to walk in step and in formation. It was a kind of "dressage" that molded the body and shaped the mind. It also included bayonet training, which was at the heart of military training, despite the development of new weapons, like the machine gun, which had made the bayonet obsolete on the battlefields of the Great War. Yet for Pershing, as for many of the generals at the time, the bayonet remained the symbol of an aggressive spirit. Hand-to-hand combat required both physical tenacity and moral fortitude, directed entirely at the adversary. "Techniques of the body," to use the concept introduced by Marcel Mauss, involving the bayonet, and broadly speaking, any sharp-edged weapon, brought out individual courage under fire. "When you drive your bayonets into those dummies out there, think of them as representing the enemy," explained an American training officer in 1917. "Think that he began the practice in this war of running bayonets through wounded, gasping-on-the-ground and defenseless prisoners. . . . So abandon all ideas of fighting them in a sportsmanlike way. You've got to hate them."[4]

1
Obstacle courses were part of the physical training that recruits received, here in Camp Wadsworth, South Carolina. Invented by Frenchman George Hébert in the early twentieth century, this type of training was introduced to the United States by Joseph E. Raycroft, from Princeton University, with the goal of improving infantrymen's endurance and self-confidence.

2
Military parades were one of the main rituals performed as soldiers bade farewell and went to war. They demonstrated the transformation of civilians into fighters and showcased a collective identity, as in this photo, with the men of the 312th Infantry Regiment on the main street of Newark, New Jersey, in 1918.

1 Christopher Capozzola, *Uncle Sam Wants You. World War I and the Making of the Modern American Citizen*, Oxford and New York, Oxford University Press, 2008, p. 8. 2 Jennifer D. Keene, *Doughboys, the Great War and the Remaking of America*, Baltimore and London, The Johns Hopkins University Press, 2001, p. 10. 3 *Home Reading Course for Citizen-Soldiers*, October 1917, p. 12. 4 Cited by Jennifer D. Keene, *World War I. The American Soldier Experience*, Lincoln, University of Nebraska Press, 2011, p. 52.

2

The American government introduced a draft, called "Selective Service," in the spring of 1917, to form an Army to fight in Europe. On July 20, 1917, Secretary of War Newton D. Baker, blindfolded, drew the number for the first group of draftees called to serve. In the 4,647 districts, men with the number 258 were the first to join their regiments. A similar ceremony was held when the second draft was launched in June 1918.

1

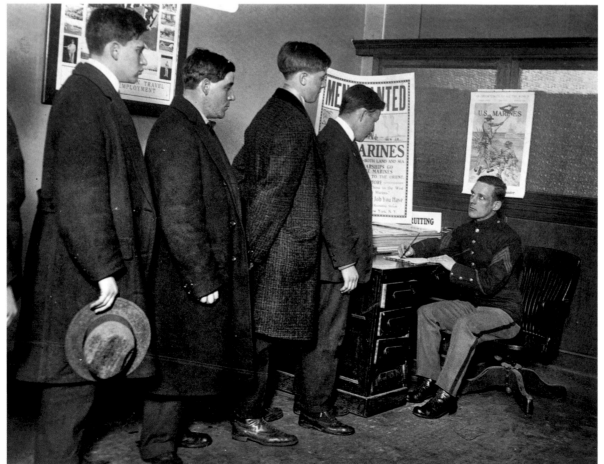

On the eve of America's entry into the war, the Marine Corps had only 15,000 men. In June 1917, General Pershing created the 1st Infantry Division by combining, contrary to tradition, infantrymen from the Regular Army and the 5th Regiment of Marines. The Marine Corps served with distinction, notably in the Battle of Belleau Wood, in June 1918.

1
This photograph, used by recruitment offices in 1918, illustrates the force of the collective spirit in the elite corps of the U.S. military. The men form a compact group around the flag, which depicts the emblems of the Marine Corps: an eagle, globe, and anchor.

2
While the Marine Corps did not allow any African Americans among their ranks throughout the entire conflict, nearly three hundred women joined, working as secretaries for the military command. In Boston, three young women, Mrs. Harold C. Daniels, Mrs. John Q. Adams and Mrs. Charles T. Owens, enlisted in 1917.

3
The Marine Corps attracted many volunteers in 1917 and 1918, like these young men crowding into the New York recruitment office. By the end of the war, the Corps had nearly 70,000 men, five times more than in 1914.

1

2

3

1-2-3-4

For most American families, the war began in train stations. This is where the men said goodbye, as they headed to training camps before traveling to the ports on the East Coast for transit to Europe. Photographs printed in newspapers highlighted the patriotic determination of the new recruits, as in this scene in a New York suburb (4). The panel, carried by a draftee still in civilian dress, states: "Express Woodhaven to Berlin, no sleepers." Trivializing the war in this way, depicting it as a vacation getaway, made it easier for both civilians and soldiers to accept the radical new experience of war, not by glorifying it, but by making it part of a familiar world. At the same time, the photographs also captured the familial, nearly intimate dimension of the mobilization. The conscripts were not only portrayed as citizens doing their duty, but also as fathers, husbands, and sons setting out to defend their own families on the battlefields of Europe (1, 2, and 3). The images of these farewells prefigured another form of mobilization, that of the domestic sphere on the home front.

4

1

1-2
Once they reached their training camps in the United States, the conscripts underwent a physical transformation, which involved training in the use of bayonets (1)—a weapon that was ill suited to the new reality of trench warfare, but which was still imbued with powerful symbolic value. With bayonets, the war is a fight between individuals. Soldiers push forward, both physically and morally, toward their adversaries. The use of a blade reinforced the manly-military model that was being superceded at this time by industrial-scale warfare and mass killings. It also developed quick thinking, an ability to instantly respond to orders from superiors, and an aggressiveness that General Pershing considered to be an essential characteristic when the Western Front shifted back to a war of movement. This modeling of the masculine body also bolstered a soldier's sense of belonging to a unit. In this bird's-eye view, a group of doughboys (2), knapsacks on their backs as they wait to ship out to Europe, illustrates the collective aspect of the war experience. After several weeks of training, the men were an integral part of the young Army of the United States.

OVER THERE

On June 14, 1917, some fifteen transport ships carrying soldiers left
New York in a thick fog, heading for France. The men of the 1st Infantry Division, known as The Big Red One, landed twelve days later in
Saint-Nazaire and joined a camp set up on the outskirts of the town.
Military equipment and soldiers later disembarked in the port of
Brest, which had a deeper harbor and could handle larger ships, and
in La Pallice and Bordeaux. American soldiers sent to England to train
with the British Army landed in Le Havre. In each of these ports, the
arrival of the Americans required a massive increase in housing facilities and a reorganization of the urban space. The docks had to be
expanded, dockworkers hired quickly, warehouses had to be built,
and rail lines laid down. By late 1918, 2 million soldiers had been transported to Europe on more than 1,000 ships, an impressive feat that
would have been impossible without the British fleet, which provided
half of the ships. An equally considerable effort was made in terms of
supplies. On average, the supply of goods for the U.S. Army increased
from 26,000 tons per month in late 1917 to 236,000 tons per month
by late 1918. Yet shipments of provisions, livestock, and raw materials
across the Atlantic Ocean did not start with America's official entry
into the conflict—a reality overlooked for many years by historians,
who tended to downplay America's global role prior to 1917.

More than 500,000 horses, for example, or one-third of those
used by the French Army during World War I, came from the United
States.[1] Purchases began in late 1914, in the wake of the disaster of
the Battle of the Frontiers (August 20–24, 1914) and the Battle of
the Marne (September 6–10, 1914), where most of the French horses
that had been mobilized at the beginning of the war perished. But
even after the war transitioned from a war of movement to trench
warfare on the Western Front, the armies still needed large numbers of horses, particularly draft horses. In November 1915, missions
sent to the United States to acquire horses for the French Army
were importing up to 33,000 per month, with about 1,000 animals shipped on each boat. They were often transported in deplor-

The first troops of the American
Expeditionary Forces, traveling aboard
several transport ships—*Havana,
Saratoga, Seattle, Neptune*—landed in
France in late June 1917. The several
thousand men, captured in perfect
alignment along the docks in official
photographs, made a powerful
impression on the local population. Yet
there was no enthusiasm in the streets
of Saint-Nazaire. "All the women seem
to be in mourning," recalled young
George Marshall, who would become
General Pershing's aide-de-camp.

1

able conditions. Once they reached the French ports, dockworkers started by removing the carcasses of animals that had died during the trip. Cranes then hoisted the horses from the ships using belly-straps. A young farmer from the Beauce region later described the sight: "Thousands of horses. They had been hot in the bottom of the holds. They were sent to barracks, half of which were out in the open in the middle of winter. It was incredible how many died."[2]

In June and July, 1917, several photo feature stories covered the landing of the doughboys and their installation in the Villès-Martin camp, near Saint-Nazaire. The images captured by the Section Photographique et Cinématographique de l'Armée give an idea of the visual shock that European civilians must have felt on seeing the American regiments land, with thousands and thousands of young soldiers lined up along the docks in French ports. The feminist author Vera Brittain, who served as a nurse in Étaples (Pas-de-Calais), watched them go by, "so much like gods, so splendid, so magnificently intact compared to the exhausted and stressed men of the British Army."[3] Yet the impression left on the local population was mixed: "They imagine that they are on conquered land. They spend money much too quickly. They chase after the girls and women too much." An American correspondent acknowledged as much in a letter to his family: "Crude, impolite and rude, the ordinary soldiers drink beer straight from the bottle and are generally very loud, so much so that for the French soldier, they have earned the name of "Pull hanks": "loudmouths."[4] We also have to imagine the sounds that accompanied the arrival of the American troops: the soldiers calling out to each other on the streets in English; the racket of the military vehicles, at a time when there were very few French cars on the road; and the sounds of a new type of music, jazz, introduced in December 1917 by the regiment band of one of the most famous conductors in New York: Lieutenant James Reese Europe. Or the neighing by unknown races of horses that came from the Great Plains of America, which locals called "Yanks." Edgy after the Atlantic crossing, the American horses were impressive in their size and in their extreme state of agitation. "These beasts bolt like cows, bite like dogs, rear up, and pull back when you want to get them moving forward."[5]

Gradually, the entire town was transformed with the installation of the Allied troops. The Pontanézen district in Brest became an American enclave, with its own hospital, theater, stores, and nearly 1,200 barracks. The residents of Saint-Nazaire, Nantes, and Le Havre had to get accustomed to the sight of these often exuberant soldiers, recognizable by their wide-brimmed felt hats, strolling in small groups through their streets. Everyday life was totally changed, not only in the port cities, but in towns and even villages throughout western France. Gièvres, a small town in the Loir-et-Cher *département*, was home to the largest American warehouse for refrigerated meat, built to supply the troops. Where there once stood a forest, "there now rises a city of wood and canvas. On the road, there's a constant flow of automobiles, side cars zooming by in a flash," described one individual. "At every intersection were ramrod-straight policemen, revolvers on their hips, wood batons in hand, maintaining order with a word, a whistle, a restrained gesture. An infinite variety of goods was constantly entering the barracks, arriving directly from one of the Atlantic ports, as well as leaving, heading for the front or the American training camps."

For the first soldiers who reached Europe, the summer of 1917 was a time of adaptation. Letters and newspapers about the war reflected their surprise as they discovered "an old, picturesque country," "filled with old people and women dressed in black." Many patriotic ceremonies, parades, and festivals alternated with training periods in weaponry and trench warfare. The most memorable of these celebrations took place when General Pershing arrived in France. On June 13, the head of the American Expeditionary Forces landed, with his staff, in the port of Boulogne-sur-Mer. Several hours later, he reached the Gare du Nord in Paris and was greeted by Marshall Joffre and the Minister of War, Paul Painlevé. The streets along the entire route of the parade taking him to the Hôtel Crillon were draped in American flags. The pediment of the Madeleine Church was covered with star-studded white bunting. The following day, Pershing visited the Invalides to pay homage to Napoleon and to see the trophies of war that had been taken from the Germans since the outbreak of hostilities. Accompanied by General Dubail, the military governor of Paris, he then went to Le Bourget Airport, where he met with French and American pilots.

The second part of the official program was aimed at strengthening bonds with French authorities. On July 14, Pershing was received by the Chambre des Députés, where René Viviani strongly praised the Franco-American friendship. The Vice-President of the Conseil des Ministres had just returned from a three-week mission in the United States, accompanied by Marshal Joffre, where he sought to win over public opinion and assess the extent of American military participation. The two men met with President Wilson and made a triumphant cross-country tour. "It was not only the recognition vis-à-vis France, in memory of the glorious services rendered by

2

3

Lafayette . . . which touched the American soul to its core; it was also the silence, the dignity, the peace of mind of France during its ordeals." Viviani then cited an American diplomat speaking to the French people: "We have always loved you; after the Marne, we admired you; since Verdun, we have respected you." On June 16, Pershing visited General Pétain, Commander-in-Chief of the armies in the north and northeast, at the Supreme Command headquarters in Compiègne. Ten days later, he would be in Saint-Nazaire to greet the men of the 1st Infantry Division, who were among the first American soldiers to set foot on French soil.

Pershing's entire trip to France can be viewed as a celebration of the historic links between France and the United States. For the Fourth of July, the American delegation went to the Picpus Cemetery in the 12th *arrondissement* of Paris, where Marquis de Lafayette is buried. This hero of the American Revolution had returned to the United States in 1825, invited by President James Monroe. At the end of his trip, he dug up dirt from the Bunker Hill battlefield, near Boston, and took it back to France, so that when the time came, he would be buried in American soil. It was this dirt that was poured on his coffin, in 1834. On July 4, 1917, Pershing was at the Picpus Cemetery, but it was one of his deputies, Lieutenant Colonel Charles E. Stanton, who spoke: "Here and now, in the presence of the illustrious dead, we pledge our hearts and our honor in carrying this war to a successful issue." And then, turning toward the tomb, he ended with these famous words, which were later reproduced on multiple propaganda posters: "Lafayette, we are here!"

1 Gene Tempest, *The Long Face of War. Horses and the Nature of Warfare in the French and British Armies on the Western Front*, doctoral thesis, Yale University, 2013, chapter 2. **2** Ephraïm Grenadou and Alain Prévost, *Grenadou, paysan français*, Paris, Éditions du Seuil, 1966, p. 77. **3** Vera Brittain, *Testament of Youth: An Autobiographical Study of the Years 1900-1925*, London, 1978, pp. 420–21. **4** Jean Nicot, *Les poilus ont la parole. Lettres du front (1917-1918)*, Brussels, Éditions Complexe, 1998, pp. 429–30. **5** Lieutenant F. de la Quintinie, *Mon journal. Notes prises au jour le jour pendant la campagne 1915–1919*, cited by Gene Tempest, *The Long Face of War, op. cit.*

3-4
In his memoirs, General Pershing described his arrival in Paris on June 13, 1917, several days before the first American soldiers landed in the port of Saint-Nazaire: "The trip was organized so that we arrived in the evening, after the workshops and offices had closed; the population could then join in the improvised welcoming events. What we wanted is for the residents to see the Americans arriving with their own eyes." Parisians surrounded the car of the commander of the American Expeditionary Forces on Place de la Concorde (3). People were so enthusiastic that the general had to step out on the balcony of the Hôtel Crillon to greet the crowd (4).

4

1

2

1-2

1-2

The Americans landed in Brest on
November 12, 1917. The Pontanézen
neighborhood—nicknamed "Ponty" by
the Sammies—was transformed into a
massive military camp that would
house more than 90,000 men, the
equivalent of the town's entire
population. The photo feature story by
Edmond Famechon in September 1918
described the everyday lives of the
Allied troops in the Brittany port, over
which the American flag flew (2). A
sailor chatting with an old woman on
the docks (1). In the background,
Vauban's citadel overlooks the Bay of
Brest.

A group of American soldiers photographed on the bridge of the ship transporting them to France, before disembarking. "With their dark olive uniforms, their wide-brimmed hats, their belts with multiple pouches, looking like young cowboys from the American West, [the doughboys] brought an unusual picturesque note to the backdrop of our war" (*L'Illustration*).

1-2

Onlookers crowd the quays of Saint-Nazaire to see the arrival of the first ships from New York (1). The silhouette of a woman in mourning stands out from the crowd. "[The Americans] arrived haloed in seductive appeal and wrapped in the fabulous prestige our roaming imaginations have always held for distant people and objects," explained a journalist. "We welcome them as if they were family and therefore we seem to see them as relatives. . . . Their pockets are full of dollars they spread lavishly. . . . They are as numerous as the stars under the auspices of which they march. . . . They bring us airplanes by the hundreds and hundreds of thousands. . . . It seems like all they have to do is swap their large soft-brimmed hats for a solid steel helmet." African-American soldiers, initially banned from fighting units, were tasked with unloading ships (2). "An American landing in France was followed by ten tons of goods slated for his upkeep, food, and weapons for one year," vaunted French war propaganda.

1

2

General Pershing went to Saint-Nazaire on June 26, 1917 to greet the first soldiers of the American contingent. He is seen here leaving the station before heading to the harbor. Born in 1860, the general already had a distinguished career behind him in Cuba, the Philippines, and Mexico. In the spring of 1917, he took over as commander of the American Expeditionary Forces in France. An outspoken supporter of the independence of the American military in relation to the Allied Command, he successfully and rapidly modernized the U.S. Army during the Great War.

1

 1-2-3

This photo feature story, taken in the Villès-Martin Camp near Saint-Nazaire in early July 1917, focused on the doughboys' equipment. For the French, the distinguishing characteristic of the American soldier was first of all his wide-brimmed campaign hat, swapped for combat duty for the flat helmet borrowed from the British Army. They wore a fabric belt fitted with ammunition pouches outside their peacoats and, on their backs, a knapsack (1); a non-commissioned officer displays its contents in one of the photographs (2): a tent, two blankets, a shovel, a mess tin and canteen, a pair of underwear, two pairs of socks, one spare pair of shoes, a towel, soap, a toothbrush, and various kitchen utensils. The French infantrymen learned from the start of the war that their knapsacks served a crucial purpose, as they contained all the implements essential to life in the trenches. But for the young American recruits, the knapsack was still a strange object; they needed to spend a long time training, learning how to pack and unpack them. When it rained, the soldiers were wrapped in long raincoats (3), which also covered their knapsacks. In the rainy summer at the training camp, doughboys learn how to cope with mud.

1

1-2
The memory of Marquis de Lafayette is closely linked to the history of the American involvement in 1917. On June 14, General Pershing paid a visit to the pilots of the Lafayette Escadrille (1) at Le Bourget Airport. On July 4, he went to the Picpus Cemetery to pay his respects to the hero of American independence (2). "Of all the great Frenchmen, he is the one we know best. Our children learn to link his name to that of Washington," the American ambassador to France would explain later. "When our armies crossed the ocean to defend the freedom that France herself had conquered, they were only trying to repay a sacred debt."

2

1

1

Joint celebrations between France and the United States were held on July 4, 1917 and 1918. Here, American troops parade in front of a statue of George Washington, Place d'Iéna in Paris, on Independence Day, 1918.

2

The mobilization of children at war adopted multiple forms. Boys from the local school on Rue Riquet in Paris celebrated American Independence Day, July 4, 1917, by draping their classroom with American flags.

2

THE POLITICS OF RACE

When the draft was introduced in the spring of 1917, African Americans were also called up to serve their country. This decision was controversial in a country still scarred by segregation, lynching, and racial violence, and was openly contested by representatives from the southern states. Considering the very idea that an African American could be the equal of a soldier citizen was a "monstrosity," Senator James K. Vardaman from Mississippi predicted that drafting blacks would trigger the "final disaster, the fall and death of our civilization." In 1915, fear of the domestic enemy was for a time directed at the black community in Texas, suspected of helping Mexican immigrants prepare for an invasion of the southern states, with help from Germany. That same year saw the release of D. W. Griffith's film *The Birth of a Nation*, which advanced a racist vision of American history and presented the Ku Klux Klan as a rampart against the growing emancipation movements. Yet in 1917 and 1918, more than 367,000 black soldiers served in the armed forces; 200,000 of them were sent to France and 40,000 were directly involved in combat.

Approximately 100,000 African Americans of draft age managed to avoid conscription. Certain civil rights campaigners, like Asa Philip Randolph and Marcus Garvey, urged civil disobedience, considering that the war was above all a conflict among imperialist powers. It was relatively easy for men living in rural areas of the Deep South to avoid military authorities or lie about their age, as birth certificates or identity papers were often lacking. Yet a major migration was underway all over the United States. Spurred by the unemployment crisis in rural southern states, thousands of African Americans moved to large industrial cities in the north: Chicago, Detroit, Pittsburgh, and New York, where salaries were higher. Those who enlisted believed they would have a better life with the 30 dollars a month the Army paid. Others hoped that the ideals of liberty, set forth as the goal of the war against Germany, would end up improving their standard of living; while still others saw the mobilization as a test, a way to prove they were members of the national community. In the National Association for the Advancement of Colored People (NAACP) magazine, historian and civil rights

African-American volunteers ready to enlist in the 8th Infantry Regiment, in Chicago, in the spring of 1917. Renamed the 370th Infantry Regiment during the war, this unit was the only one entirely under the command of black officers. Chicago already had a strong black community of around 40,000 people on the eve of the war. Fifty thousand African Americans moved to the city between 1916 and 1920, as part of the Great Migration from the southern states.

campaigner W.E.B. Du Bois wrote that Germany's militarism was as inhuman as the persecution of the black communities: "Back of the German mask is the grinning skeleton of the Southern slave driver."[1]

Yet hopes for social emancipation through military involvement were short-lived. After they were inducted, draftees were generally sent to camps reserved for African Americans, even though, in certain cases, organizations such as the YMCA maintained joint recreational activities. During their military training, black soldiers sometimes endured miserable daily lives, living in overpopulated barracks and abysmal sanitary conditions. Stationed in Camp Travis, in Texas, soldier Stanley Moore provided a glimpse in a letter to his sister: "I can't say that I like the Army life, it is a hard life to live and they are so mean to the colored boys here. They curse and beat them just like they were dogs and a fellow can't even get sick. Oh! It is an awfully mean place. I will be glad when they send me away from here."[2] Segregation extended even to the functions performed by the conscripted men. Soldiers of color were nearly always assigned to support units, troop transport, supply units, and the construction of military camps and railway lines. In the ports of embarkation to Europe, as in the French ports of Brest, Saint-Nazaire, and Bordeaux, they were responsible for handling goods and equipment. Combat duty, as least initially, was viewed as the prerogative of white men.

At the same time, there was an upsurge in racial violence in the United States. On July 2 and 3, 1917, riots claimed some one hundred victims in East St. Louis, an industrial town in Illinois. Fear of an uprising by black communities grew several weeks later, during street battles that pitted men from the 24th Infantry Regiment against white residents and the local Houston police force. In this context of rising tension, the news of the arrest of a black soldier on August 23, 1917, sparked a powder keg. Several hundred of his fellow soldiers, who were supervising the construction of Camp Logan, organized a raid in the streets of Houston. They besieged the police station and killed seventeen white civilians. Military authorities immediately suppressed the rebellion: 156 black soldiers were court-martialed, 54 were found guilty, and 13 were hanged in December of 1917, followed by six other executions after two later trials. The Houston riots triggered a massive mobilization by white supremacists, who opposed drafting African Americans, but also by black civil rights campaigners, who were calling for an end to segregation in military training.

Because the war in France needed more and more men, the War Department decided to create two infantry divisions of black soldiers,

the 92nd and the 93rd, which included nearly 40,000 soldiers. The 92nd (the Buffalo Soldiers) played a limited role at the start of the Meuse-Argonne Offensive in the fall of 1918. Its poor performance, attributable to a lack of training and mediocre commanders, was stigmatized by the U.S. military command as a sign that black soldiers were unfit for combat. The 369th, 371st, and 372nd Infantry Regiments, forming the 93rd Infantry Division, were exemplary. Placed under French command by General Pershing, wearing French uniforms, and carrying French rifles, the three units would receive the Croix de Guerre, the highest French military distinction, in recognition of their outstanding bravery.[3] These successes by black soldiers on the battlefield stirred demands by civil rights advocates in the United States, notably in New York, home to men of the 369th Infantry Regiment, known as the "Harlem Hellfighters."[4]

In letters sent home to their families in the United States, black soldiers wrote bitterly that they were treated better by the French than by the U.S. Army. In their view, France was color blind, something of an inverted reflection of their own country. "The French don't care about issues of race," wrote an American in a letter to his mother. "They treat us so well that I have to look in a mirror to remind myself that I'm black."[5] This vision overlooked the overt racism toward Senegalese riflemen and laborers from colonies who came to work in the war industry. But for the French civilian population, the black soldiers were different. They praised their kindness and politeness—qualities that set them apart, in the eyes of these same civilians, from the other American soldiers, who were criticized for their arrogance. Another black officer wrote: "One merchant in St. Dié told a field officer in our Division . . . that 'the white soldiers come into my store and throw their money at me, but the black soldiers act as if it were a pleasure to trade with me and it is they that I welcome.'"[6] The experience of the war in Europe was like a social mixing pot for everyone: black and white soldiers were billeted in the same villages, shopped at the same stores, flirted with the same women. Black soldiers were outraged that white soldiers spread rumors accusing them of being murderers and rapists.[7] A sailor stationed in Brest had a clear response to these slanderous comments: he carried around a photograph of a lynching and used it to explain the reality of racial violence in his country to incredulous French people.[8]

The work carried out by the Section Photographique et Cinématographique de l'Armée illustrates the ambiguity of the French toward black soldiers—a combination of curiosity and condescen-

3

sion. Stories show the happy faces, wide smiles, and the expression of a seeming naïveté in the face of the new reality of war. They echoed the racial stereotypes of the supposed inherent characteristics of black American soldiers—optimism, humor, simplicity—while showcasing the picturesque aspect of them being in Europe, through various themes: sports, notably boxing matches, along with dance and music. With the arrival of the African Americans, the French discovered new sounds, rhythms, and music; jazz. For a band leader like James Reese Europe, who headed up the 369th Infantry Regiment band, the battle for the emancipation of the blacks had to be fought both in the Army and in American society. He had been combating the geographic and economic segregation that affected black musicians in the city of New York for many years; he had been able to take black music beyond the ghetto of Harlem and promote it among the city's cultural elite. In December 1917, he landed in Brest with his regiment and started a tour throughout France. In spring of 1918, James Europe and his men were sent to the front lines. By mid-November, the Harlem Hellfighters would be the first American unit to reach the Rhine.

1 W. E. B. Du Bois, Editorial, *The Crisis*, 1917, 14 (1), pp. 7–10. 2 Jennifer D. Keene, *Doughboys, the Great War and the Remaking of America*, Baltimore and London, The Johns Hopkins University Press, 2001, p. 101. 3 Frank E. Roberts, *The American Foreign Legion: Black Soldiers of the 93rd in World War I*, Annapolis, Md.: Naval Institute Press, 2004. 4 Stephen L. Harris, *Harlem's Hell Fighters: The African-American 369th Infantry in World War I*, Washington DC, Brassey's, Inc., 2003. 5 Tyler Stovall, *Paris Noir: African Americans in the City of Light*, Boston, Houghton Mifflin, 1996. 6 W. E. B. Du Bois, "The Black Man and the Wounded World," ch. 14, cited by Jennifer D. Keene, *Doughboys, the Great War and the Remaking of America*, op. cit., p. 126. 7 Arthur E. Barbeau and Florette Henri, *The Unknown Soldiers: African-American Troops in World War I*, op. cit., p. 143. 8 Jennifer D. Keene, *World War I. The American Soldier Experience*, Lincoln, University of Nebraska Press, 2011, p. 104.

3
The first African-American soldiers arrive in Camp Upton, on Long Island (New York), in September 1917. With a capacity for 18,000 men, this transit camp was created in the spring of 1917 to house conscripts as they awaited transport from the port of Hoboken.

4
Court martial for the black soldiers of the 24th Infantry Regiment who participated in the Houston riot on August 23, 1917, during which seventeen white civilians lost their lives. With 156 defendants, "the largest murder trial in the history of the United States" (as written on the photograph) ended with thirteen men sentenced to hang. Six other death sentences were handed down during two subsequent court martials.

Largest Murder Trial in the History of the United States.
Scene during Court Martial of 64 members of 24th. Infantry U.S.A.
on trial for mutiny and murder of 17 people at Houston Tex. Aug 23, 1917.
Trial Held in Gift Chapel. Ft Sam Houston.
Trial Started --- Nov 1, 1917- Brig Genl. George K. Hunter. Presiding.
Col. J. A. Hull- Judge Advocate.   Counsel for Defense.
Maj. D. V. Sutphin, Asst.   ..   Maj. Harry S. Grier.
Prisoners guarded by 19th. Infantry. Co. "C" Capt. Carl J Adler
This photo Copyrighted by. W. C. Lloyd. San Antonio Tex. Reproduction not allowed.

4

1

1-2

James Reese Europe (1), band leader for the 369th Infantry Regiment, introduced the European public to ragtime and jazz during the Great War. Born in Mobile, Alabama, Europe moved to New York in 1904, where he was unable to play with symphony orchestras, which banned African Americans. In 1910, he created the Clef Club, a labor exchange, entertainment venue, and social club for African Americans, and made the first album recorded by a black orchestra, just before the outbreak of the war. He also performed a legendary concert at prestigious Carnegie Hall in 1912. In 1916, he was tasked with creating the band for New York's newly formed black regiment of the National Guard. One year later, this regiment left for Europe. His musicians (2), from New York and Puerto Rico, included Noble Lee Sissle on the violin; Russell Smith, who would become one of the most famous trumpet players of the 1920s; and Herb Flemming, who had a successful international career as a trombonist. James Reese Europe's band made a triumphant tour throughout France, before heading to combat on the front lines. For their bravery, the Harlem Hellfighters unit received the French Croix de Guerre.

1

1-2
The French Army cameramen drew on
the same visual codes to photograph
African-American soldiers as they used
for their country's colonial troops. They
highlighted exotic aspects and the
supposed inherent characteristics of the
black soldiers, such as physical strength
and a certain innate happiness. This
photograph of two soldiers playing
checkers (2), taken by Auguste Goulden
in Villers-le-Sec (Marne *département*)
captures them taking a break from war.
The image of the dancing soldier (1) is
related to the popular success of
roller-skate dancing in the 1910s.

A boxing match between two black soldiers in a French village, in 1918. Boxing offered an opportunity for social advancement and was a popular entertainment in the United States. In a deeply segregated country, black boxers could fight white boxers, but were banned from the most prestigious heavyweight category. Jack Johnson's victory over white boxer James J. Jeffries in 1910 triggered race riots.

1

1-2
This portrait taken by photographer
Maurice Boulay, in the Avocourt sector
of the Meuse *département*, depicts a
camaraderie that would have shocked
the American public (1). The smiling
French infantryman does not
demonstrate any type of superiority
over his fellow African-American
soldier, who stands slightly behind him.
With a rifle on his shoulder, the black
soldier is portrayed as a combatant, not
as a member of a support unit—an
assignment that was the lot of many
African Americans during the war. The
daily life of another black soldier in the
trenches is captured in front of a
dugout as he changes his pair of shoes
(2).

2

INITIATION

On March 21, 1918, around 4am, German assault troops attacked between Arras and the Oise. General Ludendorff had just launched an offensive he hoped would decisively break through the front and achieve a final victory. Despite advancing nearly 38 miles in certain sectors, the Michael Offensive was stopped on April 4. New attacks would follow in late May, with yet another one in early June, before the Allied Forces began a counteroffensive that would lead to the armistice. Military historians have thoroughly analyzed this reversal in the balance of power. Was Ludendorff's failure inevitable? Which factors contributed to the Allied victory: a lack of equipment, which prevented the Germans from optimizing their breakthrough in the spring of 1918; the gradual breakdown in troop morale; the superiority of French and British weaponry; or American military intervention in the conflict?

In fact, when Ludendorff began the offensive in the spring of 1918, few American troops had yet reached the Western Front. The first contingents of the American Expeditionary Forces started landing in the ports of Saint-Nazaire and Brest in the summer of 1917. Another several months were required to complete the training they had begun in the United States. At first, the weapons were supplied by the Allies: the Chauchat light machine gun, the Hotchkiss machine gun, the 75 mm field gun, Renault light tanks. At the same time, the Sammies' uniforms changed. In June 1917, with cotton uniforms and belts featuring multiple pouches, they looked like young cowboys from the American West. Wool trousers, which were better suited to bad weather, were later introduced. In combat zones, the wide-brimmed felt hats were replaced by more protective flat helmets, modeled after the British design.

The feature stories produced by the Section Photographique et Cinématographique de l'Armée illustrate the slow initiation of young Americans into their role as fighters. Images show them, under the supervision of French instructors, learning how to dig trenches, launch grenades, assemble a machine gun, fire a rifle, and aim a piece of artillery. It's impossible to look at these photographs with-

An American unit taking a break along a country road in March 1918. It was cold; the men, stuffed into their wool uniforms, are sitting in the ditch. During the Great War, infantrymen had to walk long distances. The fatigue endured as a result of these interminable marches added to the other physical and moral ordeals of the conflict.

1

1
A Franco-American film and
photographic crew in July 1917, at the
Villès-Martin Camp near Saint-Nazaire.
At the time, war photography was still
very different from what it would
become during the Spanish Civil War
and World War II: the military status of
the cameramen was uncertain, while
the weight of their equipment and
technical capabilities limited the scope
of their work along the front. It was
nearly impossible to film actual
fighting.

2
Pilots from the Lafayette Escadrille
N 124, with their heavy jumpsuits to
withstand the cold at high altitudes, at
the aviation camp in Luxeuil-les-Bains,
in May 1916.

out remembering the controversy over integrating American soldiers into the Allied armies. The French and British had proposed leaving tactical commands to junior American officers, while retaining operational and strategic control. The American's refusal of this situation, in spring of 1917, was both political and symbolic. The United States was wary of the strategies implemented by their allies that had cost so many human lives. Pershing's men would remain under American command through the end of the war, but after receiving military training from French instructors: this was well documented by the Section Photographique et Cinématographique de l'Armée. Initially, French soldiers were skeptical about this "Army of extras," barely able "to drive nurses around in a car." In their letters, they accused the American soldiers of wanting "to drag out the war," because Pershing did not envisage the hostilities ending before 1919 or 1920. "Not a single French *poilu* [soldier] trusted them," summed up one fighter. "They only came to France to party."[1]

The American Expeditionary Forces arrived in France with an organization that was very different from that of the other armies. Its divisions could have up to 40,000 men, including support troops, which was twice the size of the British, French, and German divisions.[2] From a strategic standpoint, the goal was to crush German defenses by sheer numbers. From a tactical viewpoint, General Pershing maintained that soldiers had to revive their offensive outlook, develop individual aggression, and improve their skills in handling weapons. This approach, called "open warfare," was similar to the infiltration of shock troops ordered by German generals during the Battle of the Somme in 1916. But to succeed, officers had to be well trained and there had to be efficient coordination between the artillery and the infantry—something that was lacking in the young U.S. Army. The U.S. High Command had a poor grasp of the reality of war on the Western Front.

Yet the American soldiers who arrived in 1917 were not the first to reach French soil. Several thousand volunteers, including doctors, nurses, ambulance drivers, infantrymen, and pilots had already arrived. Some had opted to serve in British or Canadian regiments. Others joined the French Foreign Legion. By leaving their countries to join the war in Europe, these volunteers were challenging the neutrality of the United States. Their motivations were diverse: a reaction to the atrocities committed by the German Army in the summer of 1914, family links with France, or a thirst for adventure. More than 180 American pilots joined the French Air Force. Several dozen men formed an all-American unit, the N124 Lafayette Escadrille, created in 1916. This unit immediately became legendary. In an atrocious war that inexorably dehumanized infantrymen, the pilots maintained a unique level of prestige, displaying a combination of modern masculinity and chivalry.[3] In the collective imagination, aviation was replacing the cavalry, which was slowly disappearing. The ace pilots of the Lafayette Escadrille soon achieved international fame. Their dogfights in the sky over Verdun were celebrated in newspapers around the world, but the stories neglected to describe the reality of their experiences: the intense cold of high altitudes, fear of being burned lived, the permanent tension. But regardless of the dangers the pilots faced, for foot soldiers, aerial warfare was a kind of inaccessible dream.

Initially billeted in non-combatant sectors, the American infantry was quickly moved to the front following the German offensive in the spring of 1918. From May 28 to 31, 1918, the village of Cantigny in the Somme *département* was the theater of the first American involvement to be filmed and photographed by the Section Photographique et Cinématographique de l'Armée. Soldiers in the 1st Division, supported by French tanks and artillery, managed to hold their positions as the German assault intensified. Cantigny would be held up as an example of the tenacity of the American troops, despite their relative inexperience.[4] The battles of Château-Thierry (June 5) and Belleau Wood (June 6–25), where the Marine Corps fought with distinction, bolstered this impression. Begun on July 18, the French counteroffensive in the Aisne-Marne sector was only made possible through the involvement of several American divisions, which suffered extremely heavy losses, due to tactical weakness and misguided command efforts.

In August, Pershing took over command of the U.S. First Army, which was responsible for an immense sector along the southeast front. His goal was to reduce the Saint-Mihiel salient, which had been held by German troops since 1914, before undertaking a massive drive toward Metz. Launched on September 12, the war's first fully American offensive was a resounding success. In just a few days, the First Army broke through the enemy's positions, as they pursued a strategic retreat. More than 15,000 Germans were taken prisoner, and 450 pieces of artillery captured. The momentum of the American troops was interrupted by an agreement between Pershing and Foch, stipulating that the First Army would be sent to another sector of the front, between the Argonne Forest and the Meuse River. The reduction in the Saint-Mihiel salient therefore did not create a larger breakthrough in the German lines.

2

3

4

Only ten days separated the end of the operations against Saint-Mihiel, on September 16, and the start of the Meuse-Argonne Offensive. The American soldiers were exhausted. After making significant advances during the first days, Pershing's men met with fierce resistance from the Germans, who held a better position in the wooded area, in which they could form multiple pockets of resistance. Through the fall of 1918, the U.S. Army suffered increasingly heavy losses. Forty-five thousand men were killed or wounded during the first four days of the Meuse-Argonne Offensive, a battle in which nearly 600,000 men fought. In September and October, 1918, the Americans experienced monthly losses that were higher than the deadliest months of the Civil War and World War I.[5] The photo feature stories celebrated their sacrifice with images of military cemeteries, religious services, and more rarely, the bodies of Allied soldiers.

In all, the involvement of the U.S. Army played a considerable role in the success of the 1918 counteroffensive. By occupying the calm zones along the front, the Sammies initially freed up French and British forces, which could then be sent to more exposed sectors. The American troops then reduced the Saint-Mihiel salient and contributed to the Meuse-Argonne Offensive, suffering major losses in the process. Yet the energy and courage of the American soldiers should not mask the persistent impression of amateurism and lack of organization. Pershing had believed that a revived fighting spirit would be enough to achieve victory.[6] The American contribution to the final victory was more psychological than military. While the resources of the Central Powers were dwindling, the U.S. Army ensured a seemingly endless supply of new troops. "More and more the Kaiser must curse Christopher Columbus's discovery," exclaimed one French soldier.[7]

3
August 1916 in the Meuse *département*: an American ambulance evacuates a wounded soldier. Even before America joined the war, thousands of Americans were working as doctors, nurses, and ambulance drivers for the Allied Forces.

4
The banality of mass death: a body carried in a shroud by two black soldiers.

5
In August/September 1918, the 10th French Army and the 32nd American Division launched a major offensive in the Soissons region. Armored tanks, along with aircraft, played an increasingly important role in the last phase of the war, as with, for example, this Renault FT-17 French tank (driven by Americans) at the Valpries farm near Juvigny.

1 Jean Nicot, *Les poilus ont la parole. Lettres du front (1917-1918)*, Brussels, Éditions Complexe, 1998, pp. 428–31. 2 Jennifer D. Keene, *World War I. The American Soldier Experience*, Lincoln, University of Nebraska Press, 2011, p. 129. 3 George L. Mosse, *Fallen Soldiers. Reshaping the Memory of the World Wars*, Oxford, Oxford University Press, 1990, pp. 119–24. 4 Allan R. Millett, "Cantigny, 28–31 May 1918," *in* Charles E. Heller, edit., and William A. Stofft, ed., *America's First Battles, 1776-1965*, Lawrence, University Press of Kansas, 1986. 5 Edward G. Lengel, *To Conquer Hell: the Meuse-Argonne 1918. The Epic Battle that Ended the First World War*, New York, Henry Holt and Co., 2008. 6 David F. Trask, *The AEF and Coalition Warmaking, 1917–1918*, Lawrence, University Press of Kansas, 1993. 7 Jennifer D. Keene, *Doughboys, the Great War and the Remaking of America*, Baltimore and London, The Johns Hopkins University Press, 2001, p. 106.

5

1

1-2

The doughboys arrived in Europe
without any experience in the reality of
industrial-scale warfare. They had to
learn what Allied infantrymen had
known for several years: how to dig a
trench, rig up a shelter, lay barbed wire.
Military training took place on training
fields of military camps like this one in
Demange in the Meuse *département*, in
August 1917 (1). Instructors were
generally French and British Allied
officers. The images shot by military
cameramen depict an easygoing
atmosphere, far different from the
reality of the front. In the Mauvages
training center, an American soldier
who successfully passed his first
grenade launching test is cheered by his
comrades (2).

1

2

1-2-3
In the spring of 1917, the U.S. Army was
still ill-equipped and poorly prepared
for trench warfare. A large share of its
weaponry was supplied by the Allies, at
least through early 1918. In their
training camps, the doughboys had to
learn how to use French and English
equipment (2,) like the Hotchkiss
machine gun and the Chauchat light
machine gun. In July 1917, in
Houdelaincourt, French and American
soldiers explain how to use their
respective rifles, the Lebel and the
M1917 Enfield (1). Soldiers in training
with French instructors in the American
military camp of Tréveray, in the Meuse
département (3). These images from the
Section Photographique et
Cinématographique de l'Armée
illustrate the cooperation among the
Allied Forces and may have been
intended for publication in the press.

3

1

2

3

1-2-3
By the time the American soldiers reached France, the armies had already developed—in late 1915 and early 1916—masks fitted with cartridge filters that were effective against chemical warfare. Cameramen photographed training sessions extensively, during which soldiers had to learn how to quickly don their protection and breathe through their masks (3). This one, which covered the entire face and was attached with straps behind the head, felt suffocating to wear. It isolated soldiers from one another, making them unrecognizable, as suggested by the concerned expressions of soldiers in training, here in March 1918 (1). This anonymity, which interfered with communication among fellow soldiers on the battlefield, added to the terror of poison gas and the invisible death it caused. Masks were also invented for animals in the trenches, including dogs and horses. Here, Sergeant Joseph Levin, of the Chemical Warfare Service, with his horse, Buddy, in 1917 (2).

A fleeting glimpse of a group of
American horsemen riding through
Crézanzy, in the Aisne *département*. The
military photographers were fascinated
by the horses, perhaps because they
harked back to another era, prior to
industrial-scale warfare, when the
cavalry still played a major role.

1

1-2
Artillery pieces were one of the favorite subjects in the early phases of war photography. As symbols of military and industrial power, they were obvious choices for the visual propaganda that glorified the nation and its Army. Photographers, all men of the nineteenth century thrown into total warfare for the first time, were fascinated by these tools of massive destruction, as well as by ruins. The power of this gigantic 203-mm Howitzer, photographed in the summer of 1918 in Senoncourt, in the Meuse, can be deduced from the number of soldiers required to load the gun (1) and aim it (2): a total of twelve men in all.

2

1

1-2

By the summer of 1914, the machine gun controlled the battlefield, making it virtually impossible for infantrymen to advance without artillery support. It sent a stream of bullets toward attackers that soldiers sometimes compared to a "nest of hornets" flying overhead. It was a fairly new weapon, developed in 1884 by the Americans. Improved in 1917 and 1918, it had become lighter, like this model photographed in the summer of 1918 (1). Infantrymen's other fear was chemical warfare, despite the relatively low number of deaths it caused, at least on the Western Front. There are very few images that show as clearly as this one a cloud of gas drifting toward soldiers (2). In October 1918, the date of this attack, approximately one-quarter of the shells fired by the artillery contained toxic substances.

Following double page

In 1914–1918, it was nearly impossible to photograph or film soldiers in combat. The equipment was too cumbersome and the battlefields too dangerous for the cameramen. There are very few photographs of soldiers mounting an attack, bayonets fixed; existing images were often staged. Here, an exceptional photograph of the battle of Cantigny, in the Somme *département*, on May 28, 1918.

2

1

2

1-2
The real purpose of this ceremonial
photograph was to pay tribute to the
Allies by praising their sacrifice: the
burial of an American soldier (2) and
the commemoration, in September
1918, of the Battle of Belleau Wood, just
two months before the end of the
fighting (1). The horror of mass death
and the mutilation of bodies was kept
at bay by the perfect organization of
rituals and the participation of military
authorities. Yet the emotion is palpable,
with the presence of French civilians of
all ages at a funeral mass.

1

In contrast to the alignment of identical stones or crosses, which became the norm for military cemeteries in the 1920s, graves during the war instead sought to preserve a certain individuality. This was a tribute paid by fellow soldiers to the dead and probably a form of resistance to the anonymity of the mass killings. The wooden crosses, which marked temporary tombs, were often blanketed with flowers (2). The memory of the dead also gave rise to pilgrimages to the tombs of World War I heroes, even during the war, such as, for example, that of Lieutenant Quentin Roosevelt, the youngest son of the former American president Theodore Roosevelt, killed in aerial combat in the Aisne *département* on July 14, 1918 (1).

1

1-2

In August 1918, the small town of
Fismes, in the Marne *département*, was
the scene of fierce fighting between the
28th (Keystone) Division and German
assault troops. The Americans fought
street by street to take the town, using
flamethrowers and eluding sniper fire.
After an artillery battle, Fismes, which
had changed sides five times, was
destroyed beyond recognition. American
soldiers took photographs of themselves
on the devastated main square (1). The
image shows them stunned by the
ravages of industrial-scale warfare. In
another photograph (2), taken in
Cheppy, in the Argonne region, where a
regiment from Missouri fought, a black
soldier stands in front of panels
indicating multiple directions, notably
the YMCA, forming a striking contrast
between the military signposts and the
overall desolation. The photograph has
a simple handwritten caption: "Souvenir
de Verdun, 1918. Varennes."

APREMONT
MONTBLAINVILLE

CHEPPY

AL

TANK CORPS.
306TH BGDE

YMCA

Message Center

Town Major

VARENNES

EPINONVILLE
MONTFAUCON

CHARPENTRY

DUN-SUR-MEUSE

VOUZIERS
CHEPPY.

VERY

VERY.

Souvenir de Verdun 1918
Varennes

2

1

1

In a world overwhelmed by the sounds of war, music brought a comforting diversion to soldiers in the trenches. The doughboys arrived in France with their own musical tastes, songs, instruments, new melodies, and new rhythms. A small group of men gather around this banjo player.

2

An American soldier holding a white-nosed coati, a small mammal from Arizona and New Mexico, on a leash. Soldiers often adopted mascots to give their group a symbolic identity or merely for fun. Animals sometimes served more useful purposes: a dog could find wounded men on the battlefield, perform guard duty, and transport packages. The exotic nature of the coati clearly reminded its owner of his home, on the border between the United States and Mexico. Both share the same fate, that of exile.

1

2

1-2

Soldiers on a break wash their clothes in a river (1). Soldiers in the trenches said that wearing the same clothes for several weeks on end was one of the worst parts of the war, as bad as the close living conditions. The lack of personal hygiene meant that vermin were a constant concern. Washing clothes and bathing gave the soldiers some sense of physical comfort and dignity, at least temporarily. In the second photograph, African-American soldiers (2) are bathing: the water refreshed and cleansed their bodies, removing the stains of war.

1

2

3

1-2-3
Actual fighting occupied only a tiny
share of the soldiers' time. Troops on
the front lines were regularly sent
behind the lines, where logistics
supplies and rest camps were located.
In villages located far from the combat
zones, it was almost possible to forget
the war. American troops made friends
with civilians from whom they procured
supplies. The Section Photographique et
Cinématographique de l'Armée
promoted this familiarity between the
French and the Americans to illustrate
the friendship that existed between the
two countries. One American soldier
cradles a child (1), others chat with
villagers as they draw water from the
well (2), and flirt with French women
(3). Couples formed under the eyes of
French soldiers. "These men, wearing
their large-brimmed hats, leave an
enduring memory behind wherever
they go. They are very friendly and pay
generously . . . especially to the women
who are looking for consolation after
such a long wait," quipped one
artilleryman in a letter censored by the
postal control.

American soldiers on a hill over Aix-les-Bains gaze out at Lake Bourget at their feet: it's a meditative moment in the presence of a spectacular view, a contrast to the limited horizon of the battlefield. For these men from another continent, who could not return home, leaves gave them an opportunity to discover France, notably Paris and the Riviera. These breaks then became like tourist expeditions. Thanks to the Vest Pocket, Kodak's folding compact camera, a number of officers captured visual memories of these exceptional moments.

AMERICANS ALL

War was declared in the spring of 1917, a time when the country was in the midst of a major demographic transition. Since the 1880s, the United States had taken in nearly 20 million immigrants: Germans, Scandinavians, and Italians fleeing poverty; and Jews from Russia and Poland, victims of pogroms. Many of them were torn between links to their country of birth and allegiance to their new nation. Starting in August 1914, the German consulate in New York was flooded with requests from recent immigrants who wanted to return to Europe to fight in the German Army. Groups of reservists paraded down Broadway, while German-language newspapers called on their readers to promote the German cause among their fellow American citizens.[1] Other ethnic minorities supported the Central Powers: the Irish, for their dislike of the British; and Central European Jews, for their hatred of Russian anti-Semitism. The first challenge for the United States was to maintain national unity, given that first- and second-generation immigrants formed one-third of the American population. In April 1918, a poster for the third war loan depicted a family of immigrants who had recently arrived in the United States, with a slogan that sounded like an injunction: "Remember! The flag of liberty, support it!"

For certain communities, the war offered an opportunity to forge a shared identity. The 34,000 Italians, who accounted for one in five residents in New Haven, Connecticut, in 1917, defined themselves more in terms of the region or village they came from. World War I unified the community, which became the population that most widely supported the war in the entire town.[2] The situation of Americans from Germany and the Austro-Hungarian Empire was more difficult. In June of 1917, then in May of 1918, the authorities set up a surveillance policy, with the Espionage Act and the Sedition Act. They also sought to eliminate any German influence on American cultural life; this resulted in a ban of German literature in libraries, as

In 1917 and 1918, Arthur Mole and John D. Thomas took a series of patriotic photographs to promote the sale of war loans. This flag, formed by 10,000 sailors at the Great Lakes Training Station, in Illinois, was created by the two photographers as a "living emblem of the American union." At the time, the American flag had only forty-eight stars: Alaska and Hawaii only acquired statehood in 1959.

1

well as a ban on teaching German in schools, and performing German music in theater repertories.[3] In the German district of Columbus, Ohio's capital, Schiller, Germania, Kaiser, and Bismarck streets were renamed Whittier, Stewart, Lear, and Lansing.

Americans were encouraged to keep a close eye on their German neighbors—or those assumed to be so. On April 4, 1918, riots broke out in Collinsville, Illinois, where Robert Paul Prager, a German-born coal miner, was lynched by a mob. The eleven men suspected of murder were all acquitted one month later. The hunt for spies also resulted in multiple arrests. In March of 1918, suspicious annotations on the margins of a score of *St. Matthew Passion* were grounds enough to imprison Karl Muck, conductor of the Boston Symphony Orchestra, in Fort Oglethorpe, Georgia. He would later be deported to Europe and refused all offers to return to the United States after the war.

Ironically, Ellis Island, which had been the transit point for hundreds of thousands of immigrants in the late nineteenth century, was transformed into a prison for enemy aliens in 1917. Yet the total number of foreign-born Americans and foreigners interned from 1917 was far fewer than the 110,000 citizens of Japanese origin who were imprisoned during World War II. Loyalty was the federal government's watchword. The entry into the war was a time to reaffirm shared values and the social contract on which the United States was founded. The same messages, repeated constantly, appeared on every street and along major thoroughfares: "Do your duty," "Stay alert," "Be loyal to your country."

Those who were not mobilized were encouraged to participate in the war effort in other ways. Many Americans started working in factories that were producing weapons, munitions, explosives, trucks, and aircraft. Uniforms, hats, helmets, shoes, and boots also had to be provided to 4 million men, while supply chains to provide food to all the training camps in the United States, then to the troops sent to Europe, had to be organized. The mobilization in the spring of 1917 led to a massive conversion of factories producing consumer goods into war industries. With so many men leaving for the front, many women found themselves drawn into the workforce by a host of better-paying, more specialized jobs in the industrial sector—formerly staffed by male employees—and by increased opportunities as stenographers, secretaries, and telephone operators. With the migration of many African Americans to the north, many black women moved to industrial cities like Chicago, Detroit, and New York, where they worked as laborers or housemaids.[4]

1
With the creation of a conscript Army, the United States had to equip some 4 million men, providing them with uniforms, shoes, and boots. In the spring of 1917, the U.S. Army purchased nearly 400,000 steel combat helmets from the British to equip their own soldiers. The first helmets mass-produced in American factories, modeled after the British version, were not available until early 1918.

2
In 1917 and 1918, the mobilization and transport of men to the front meant that women stepped into jobs that had up to then been reserved exclusively to men. In the streets of major American cities, women were sometimes directing traffic. Other women delivered the mail, drove tramways, and checked tickets in train stations.

In the countryside, women whose husbands had gone to war found themselves at the head of family businesses, assisted by men who were too old to be mobilized and a few farmworkers. They received support from the 20,000 women who joined the Women's Land Army of America, created in 1917. These "farmerettes," as they were called, came mostly from cities and universities and had never worked on a farm prior to the war. They learned how to sow, plant, and harvest. On the West Coast, Berkeley students received an intensive course from the agriculture department of the University of California-Davis. The *Los Angeles Times* welcomed this "Army of women farmers" as an "event in the history of American women." Photographs from the first day of work made front-page news; in one, a young woman, compared to "an Amazon," is perched atop an enormous tractor. "Joan of Arc left the soil to save France; we're going back to the soil to save America," proclaimed the slogan of the Women's Land Army of America. For the farmerettes, this comparison between combat and fieldwork was more than just an affirmation of their contribution to the war effort. Members of the Women's Land Army of America wore uniforms, like soldiers on the front lines. Like them, they underwent a rigorous training program intended to select those who were the most physically and psychologically suited to the task. From an economic standpoint, the lack of available labor meant that they could negotiate better working conditions, salaries equal to those of men, and an eight-hour work day with their employers.

In the private sphere, American women were also encouraged to participate in the war effort. Every housewife had to sign a card on which she committed to "meatless Mondays," "wheatless Wednesdays," and heatless days to economize resources.[5] Households were compared to a battlefield on the domestic front. "Food Will Win the War," promised Herbert Hoover, who ran the U.S. Food Administration. Women would play a decisive role in the upsurge in volunteer activities set up by the Wilson administration to stimulate the war effort.[6] Red Cross volunteers alone knitted more than 22 million articles of clothing for hospitals and 15 million for the Army. The humanitarian organization collected 100,000 dollars by auctioning off the wool of sheep that grazed on the White House lawn. Other women worked in Salvation Army or YMCA canteens. Still others helped the American Library Association gather thousands and thousands of books and newspapers that were then sent to the American troops. Wives and mothers of soldiers were invited to participate in large fundraising campaigns for Liberty Bonds and war charities.

2

3

At the same time, women were increasingly making their voices heard in the public arena. In January 1915, the Woman's Peace Party, the leading pacifist organization consisting entirely of women, was formed. In the spring of 1915, several delegates traveled to the Netherlands to participate in the first International Congress of Women. The country's entry into the war divided the ranks of the feminist movement into those who continued to support peace at any price and those who wanted to support the government to promote the issue of women's suffrage. Militants who chose to oppose the war or provide legal assistance to conscientious objectors faced repression from the federal government.[7] The anarchist Emma Goldman, who had immigrated to the United States in 1885, created the No-Conscription League in 1917. Arrested in 1917, she was sentenced to two years in prison for anti-military activities and deported to Russia in 1919.

The postwar years were decisive in the fight for women's suffrage, which began with the Women's Rights Convention in 1848. The Nineteenth Amendment to the U.S. Constitution was ratified on August 18, 1920, granting women the right to vote—except for Native American women, who only obtained this right in June of 1924. However, as in other countries, many women lost their jobs when the soldiers were demobilized. They could no longer get the better-paying jobs that had been available during the war years. As opposed to the stereotype of the flapper, the liberated woman in the Roaring Twenties, most women went back to their traditional roles when peace returned. For them, the changes wrought by the war were temporary and illusory.

3

During the conflict, more than 3,000 aircraft were manufactured in Dayton, Ohio, to equip the U.S. Army. In October 1918, the Wright factory employed over 8,000 workers and managed to manufacture up to 400 aircraft per month. This photograph, depicting an airplane ready to be sent to Europe, illustrates the efficiency of the production lines in the war industries: the exact time it is shipped to the front is painted on its fuselage.

4

This image of a munitions factory, in Bethlehem, Pennsylvania, incorporates the usual style of industrial photography: a receding perspective and an alignment of machines creating the impression of strength and order. The American flags hanging from the ceiling and attached to the production lines also evoke the powerful industrial mobilization in a time of total war.

1 Ross J. Wilson, *New York and the First World War. Shaping an American City*, Ashgate, 2014, pp. 67–71.
2 Christopher M. Sterba, *Good Americans. Italian and Jewish Immigrants During the First World War*, Oxford and New York, Oxford University Press, 2003. 3 Jörg Nagler, "Victims of the Home Front. Enemy Aliens in the United States During the First World War," in Panikos Panayi, ed., *Minorities in Wartime: National and Racial Groupings in Europe, North America and Australia During the Two World Wars*, Providence R.I., Berg, 1993.
4 Maurine Weiner Greenwald, *Women, War and Work: The Impact of World War I on Women Workers in the United States*, Ithaca, N.Y., Cornell University Press, 1990. 5 Helen Zoe Veit, *Modern Food, Moral Food: Self-Control, Science and the Rise of Modern American Eating in the Early Twentieth Century*, Chapel Hill, The University of North Carolina Press, 2015. 6 Christopher Capozzola, *Uncle Sam Wants You. World War I and the Making of the Modern American Citizen*, Oxford and New York, Oxford University Press, 2008, chap. 3.
7 Kathleen Kennedy, *Disloyal Mothers and Scurrilous Citizens: Women and Subversion During World War I*, Bloomington, Indiana University Press, 1999.

4

2

In April 1917, Congress authorized the
first Liberty loan to finance the war
effort. The four Liberty Bonds and the
1919 Victory Bond raised 21 billion
dollars. One-third of all Americans
participated in this demonstration of
patriotic duty. In 1918, German-born
singer Ernestine Schumann-Heinck
toured the country to help with
fundraising efforts (1) and performed
concerts for the American troops.
Screen actors like Douglas Fairbanks,
Mary Pickford, and Charlie Chaplin were
also enlisted to help promote war
bonds (2).

1

1-2
Following the mobilization in the spring of 1917, the status of women in American society changed, mirroring events in other countries at war. Many women farmers were left to run their family farms alone once the men had been mobilized. Twenty thousand students volunteered in the Women's Land Army of America, created in 1917. In this photograph, taken during a county fair in Springfield, Massachusetts, a young woman from Vassar College in New York poses elegantly atop a tractor (1). Women also worked in war industries, manufacturing shells (2), ammunition, rifles, and aircraft. Many of them had already been in the workforce before the war. Mobilization opened the door to better-paid and more highly specialized jobs. Photographs of women at work glorified the everyday heroism of American women and the mobilization of the entire American society as the country waged total war.

1

1-2
As part of the fight against the internal enemy, thousands of people were forced to register with the American police. This measure called for taking fingerprints (1) and a photograph, and recording personal information, such as the name of family members serving in enemy armies. It applied to all men who were not citizens over the age of fourteen, and women married to foreigners. The policy of exclusion extended to the public sphere, as in this district of Chicago (2), where a group of children discover a sign reading: "Danger to pro-Germans. Loyal Americans Welcome to Edison Park."

2

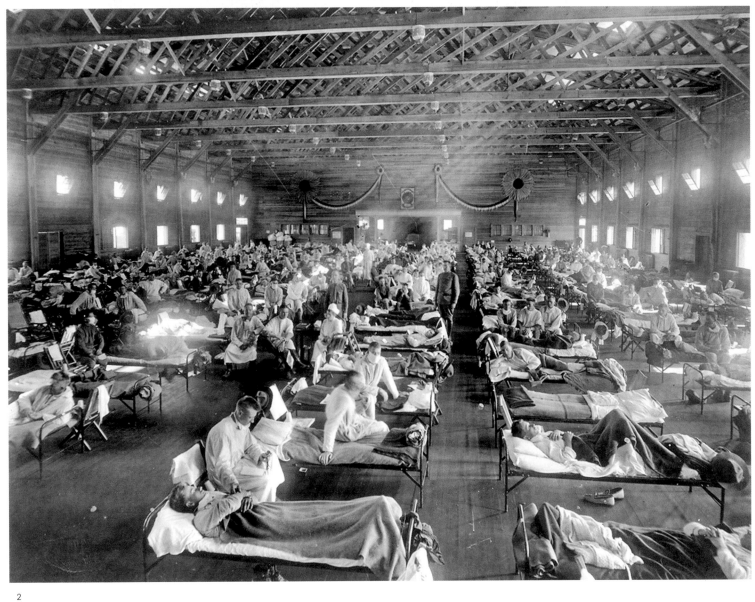

2

1-2
The first cases of the Spanish flu
appeared in the United States in March
1918, in the military hospital of Camp
Funston in Kansas (2). The pandemic,
one of the deadliest in the history of the
world, claimed at least 675,000 lives
throughout the country. A significant
number of victims who caught this
highly contagious virus were young
adults between the ages of twenty and
forty; many died two to three days after
experiencing the first symptoms. In the
absence of medication, prophylactic
measures—like soaking masks in
antiseptics (1) or spraying disinfectants
in the streets—had little effect.

THE POWER OF HUMANITARIANISM

The Great War was an unprecedented human catastrophe, for both soldiers and civilians alike. It triggered a revolution in the way that professionals and non-governmental organizations provided assistance to war victims, who became part of a global context. Humanitarian aid, in the modern sense of the term—assistance to the wounded and to prisoners, refugees, and war orphans, along with reconstruction of regions destroyed by conflict—truly emerged in the years 1914 to 1918.[1] The goal, of course, was never merely philanthropy. For a country like the United States, humanitarian actions had a political dimension from the start, as it allowed the country to intervene in the European conflict while preserving its official neutrality, through the spring of 1917. America could strengthen bonds with its European allies and hope to secure more contracts after the war and during reconstruction. Humanitarian organizations were also a way to symbolically enshrine the country's new global status. For the American people, they presented the image of an idealistic, benevolent, and "exceptionally altruistic" nation, in the words of historian David Kennedy.[2]

The first component of this humanitarian action was to provide help for the war-wounded. Starting in the summer of 1914, the American Red Cross, at the time an organization with fairly limited funds, sent medical equipment and staff to Europe.[3] The American Ambulance Hospital set up its operations in the Lycée Pasteur in Neuilly-sur-Seine. It was financed by private donors that included the Chamber of Commerce, and wealthy American families in Paris and in cities like New York, Boston, and Saint Louis, for whom a number of the hospital rooms were named. Automobile manufacturer Ford provided ten Model-T cars and drivers to be used as ambulances. Teams of doctors from Philadelphia, Cleveland, and Harvard University, including the famous neurosurgeon Harvey Cushing, provided care to the wounded in France. Everyone had to learn as quickly as possible about practicing medicine in a war situation and working with wounds that were unknown in peace time. In an article in the *American Journal of Nursing*, two young nurses described their daily lives at the American hospital as a baptism by fire: "We did not hear the bullets whistle or the cannon boom; . . . we did not hear the dying horses scream; we saw none

Official photographs sought to showcase the modern equipment and efficiency of the evacuation services, like this American Red Cross ambulance in Westouter, southwest of Ypres, in May 1918. In reality, however, picking up the wounded on the front lines and transferring them to hospitals by car or train was often a slow and inefficient process, resulting in many deaths as they were transported behind the lines.

1

Humanitarian aid played a major role in the wartime experience in the United States. Support for civilian victims raised awareness among the American population about the violence of modern warfare and shifted opinion away from President Wilson's policy of neutrality. Herbert Hoover, head of the Commission for Relief in Belgium, was a major figure in this humanitarian diplomacy. He founded a massive program to assist Belgian and French civilians living under German occupation. The businessman was considered a hero by the local population. In this photograph (2), a group of Flemish schoolchildren demonstrate their appreciation. Each one is holding a sign indicating the goods supplied by the Americans. The children also returned the empty sacks of wheat, part of the food aid, after decorating them with patriotic messages and flags. In July 1918, Hoover posed for a family portrait (1), along with thank-you letters he had received.

of the theatrical side of war; but we did get a glimpse . . . at what is its most real part. . . . we saw strong men sobbing like children in pain; we saw them crippled, dying. All these things are the necessary routine of war. We have seen, and we can never forget."[4]

Starting with the Battle of the Frontiers and the Battle of the Marne, in 1914, waves of wounded soldiers streamed into French hospitals, which were rapidly overwhelmed. An entire chain of treatment had to be organized, from first-aid stations in combat zones to hospitals behind the front. Medics on the front lines did not have enough bandages, splints, or tetanus serum. Two-thirds of the injured had shrapnel wounds, which were often contaminated by debris. Those who could be transported were evacuated farther from the front lines to undergo operations. It was a strange kind of evacuation, a chaotic rush of medical trucks and trains, stacked with stretchers. Created in early 1915, the American Fund for French Wounded sought to alleviate this health disaster by collecting clothing and medicine. Nearly 2,000 volunteers served in the American Ambulance Field Service, which worked all along the front lines, not only in France, but also in the Balkans and in Italy. Most of them were students from Yale, Princeton, and Harvard, and included future authors such as the young Ernest Hemingway, eighteen years old at the time, who drew on this experience to write *A Farewell to Arms* (1929). He was seriously injured on the Italian front during the summer of 1918. Despite his fragile health, John Dos Passos managed to join the Norton-Harjes Ambulance Corps, which was affiliated with the American Red Cross in 1917. "We had spent our boyhood in the afterglow of the peaceful nineteenth century," he wrote. "There was a war on. What was war like? We wanted to see with our own eyes."[5]

Other American volunteers helped civilian populations in German-held regions. Belgium, whose agricultural resources had been systematically looted, was the first country to suffer from famine. In October 1914, a meeting between the United States Ambassador to Belgium, Brand Whitlock, and Belgian representatives resulted in the creation of a new humanitarian agency, the Committee for Relief in Belgium (CRB), run by American businessman Herbert Hoover. Starting in April 1915 and braving the dangers of war and the Allied blockade, the organization obtained approval from the Germans, French, and British to import tons of provisions for the civilian population, first to Belgium and then to occupied regions in northern France.

The CRB, a transnational institution that was unprecedented in the history of humanitarian aid, was supported by a network of agents located around the world, from Southeast Asia to South America, who purchased rice, wheat, flour, and fodder, which was then transported to Europe aboard their own ships. This immense operation was financed by subsidies from the United States, France, Great Britain, and Belgium, with funds raised from private sources. The American delegates had passes that allowed them to travel throughout the occupied regions of Belgium and northern France. They also received help from thousands of regional committees and some seventy thousand French and Belgian volunteers, who were tasked with assessing the needs of the various populations and with distributing the humanitarian aid. By November 1918, the CRB had distributed nearly 5.7 million tons of food to more than 9.5 million French and Belgian civilians.

In the spring of 1917, the retreat of the front line liberated a number of regions that had been occupied by the Germans. The American Fund for French Wounded diversified its operations to include a "civilian section" that helped refugees and residents along the former front. Interrupted by a new German offensive, it returned to work in the spring of 1918. Ten *départements* in northern France had been invaded from 1914 to 1918. The battles devastated 7.5 million acres of farmland. At the end of the war, trenches had to be filled in, barbed wires ripped up, and shells removed. A "red zone" consisting of 450 square miles of land was declared unfit for farming or livestock: the cost of reclaiming the land would be higher than its value. Given the scope of destruction, the government had no other choice but to buy the land and reforest it.

The Americans who discovered the war-torn landscape of northern France were horrified. "You can drive for hours and see nothing but ruins," noted Anne Murray Dike. With her friend Anne Morgan, the youngest of banker John Pierpont Morgan's four children, she founded the American Committee for Devastated France, which played a crucial role in reconstruction. Anne Morgan was the mainstay of the philanthropic organization in the United States. She was the primary force behind the fundraising campaigns, drawing on modern techniques of publicity, and adapting them to the humanitarian field. She understood the role of photography to raise awareness among the public about the suffering of French civilians.[6] Full-page portraits of refugees were published in the American press. After working with the Section Photographique et Cinématographique de l'Armée, the American Committee for Devastated France put together its own film crew, which included contributions by one of the greatest American landscape painters, Harry B. Lachman, and French director Firmin Gémier. "A film is more convincing than words," said Anne Morgan, when she presented her documentary *Heritage of France* (1919), about refugees.

2

3

3

As a non-governmental organization, the American Red Cross could only operate with the help of thousands of volunteers and donations from private sources. Here, nurses and boy scouts participate in a fundraising campaign in the streets of Birmingham, Alabama, in May 1918..

4

Capturing the destructive power of industrial-scale warfare, photographs of ruined cities in northern France fascinated civilian populations located behind the front lines. They contributed to the propaganda efforts intended for the Allies and neutral countries, and were used to condemn the brutality of the enemy. They sometimes recorded attacks on national identity and the country's cultural heritage, as was the case for the Reims Cathedral and other monuments targeted by the Germans. And finally, images of ruins were used to fully document the extent of the destruction and to prepare for postwar reconstruction efforts.

Anne Murray Dike's medical training made her the obvious choice to take care of humanitarian work in the field. The volunteers in this all-female organization had to speak French, have a driver's license, and be able to support themselves. "We do not want tourists coming to France to visit the battlefields," warned Anne Morgan. These women wore sky blue uniforms, giving them a somewhat martial look. General Philippe Pétain allocated space for their headquarters in the Château de Blérancourt, just 20 miles from the front. Letters written by young Marian Grier Bartol, from a wealthy Philadelphia family, described the extravagant group of volunteers she was working with in France: "How much Father would have hated all these modern and independent young women," she admitted.[7] Their days were spent distributing food, farm equipment, seeds, livestock, and construction material.

The action of the American committee was not, however, limited to the material reconstruction of the devastated sectors. Confronted with the suffering of the refugees, the American volunteers also undertook a "moral and social reconstruction" of the region. They created day-care centers; supplied chalk, notebooks, and books to schoolchildren; and encouraged sports activities. Five public libraries were opened in the Aisne *département*, introducing an American model of operation for the first time in France that included free access to books, classification by subject, and free book loans.[8] Through the activities of these humanitarian organizations, a little bit of American culture took root in the midst of the ruins. "In our region, colors and shapes had disappeared or were so deformed that no one's imagination was ever stimulated," recalled one refugee from the former battle zone. "Life would have been boring and sterile without photographs, films, kindergartens, books."[9]

1 Annette Becker, *Oubliés de la Grande Guerre : humanitaire et culture de guerre, 1914–1918*, Paris, Noésis, 1998; new ed., Pluriel, 2003 ; Bruno Cabanes, *The Great War and the Origins of Humanitarianism, 1918-1924*, Cambridge, Cambridge University Press, 2014. 2 David M. Kennedy, *Over Here: The First World War and American Society*, Oxford, Oxford University Press, 1980, p. 153. 3 Julia F. Irwin, *Making the World Safe: The American Red Cross and a Nation's Humanitarian Awakening*, Oxford and New York, Oxford University Press, 2013. 4 "Experiences in the American Ambulance Hospital, Neuilly, France," *The American Journal of Nursing*, vol. 15, n° 7, April 1915, pp. 549–54. 5 John Dos Passos, *One Man's Initiation*, 1917, Ithaca, NY: Cornell University Press, 1969, pp. 4–5. 6 Heide Fehrenbach and Davide Rodogno, ed., *Humanitarian Photography: A History*, Cambridge, Cambridge University Press, 2016. 7 Letters of Marian Grier Bartol, Morgan Library Archives, New York. 8 Anne Dopffer, "Le Comité américain pour les régions dévastées," in *Reconstructions en Picardie après 1918*, Réunion des Musées Nationaux, 2000, pp. 70–86. 9 *Ibid.*, p. 81.

4

2

1

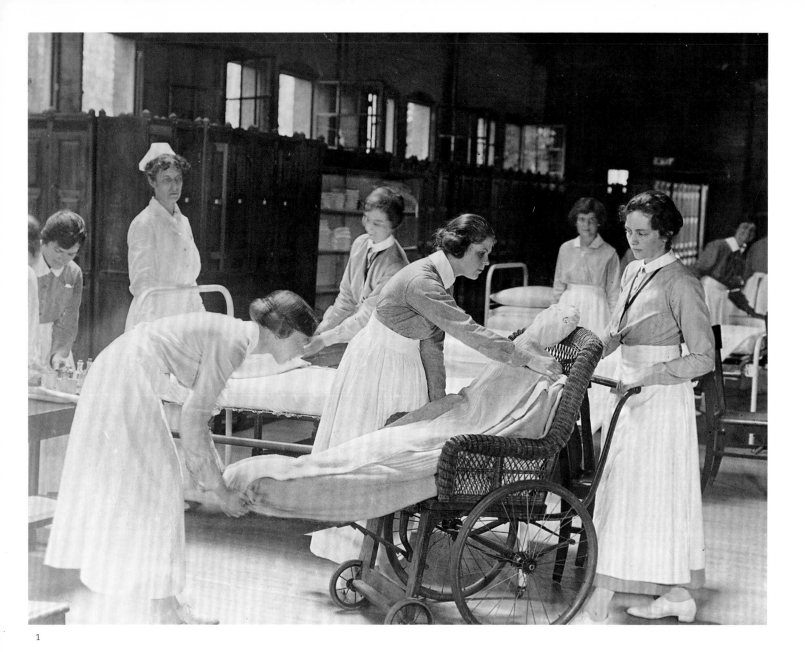

1

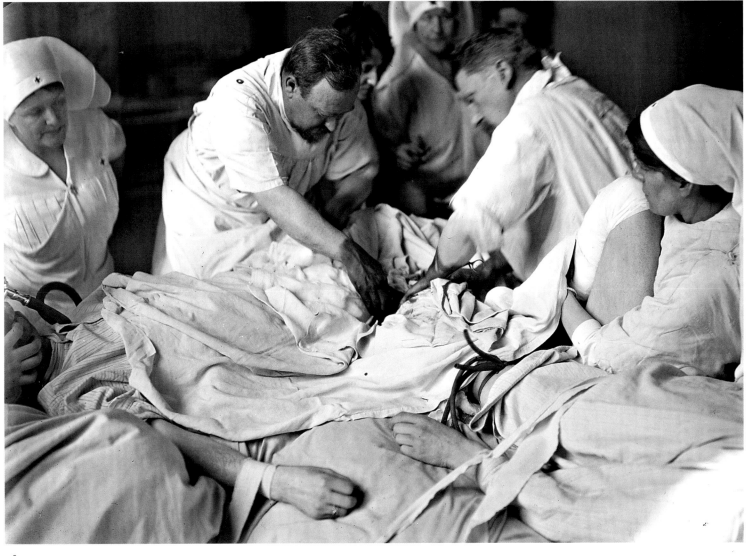

2

1-2
For women during the Great War, becoming a nurse was a way to get involved as a volunteer. After receiving practical training—like these Vassar College students learning how to maneuver a mannequin onto a stretcher (1)—some 10,000 American nurses were sent to Europe. Letters and journals written by these women, who were often young and from wealthy families, describe their shock as they first confronted the reality of war, the bodies of soldiers, and the suffering of the wounded. In an era before antibiotics, it was essential to clean wounds and change dressings to prevent infection. Working under a male hierarchy, nurses never had autonomous authority and were limited to providing medical assistance, particularly during surgical procedures (2).

1

1-2
Even before the United States joined the war, millions of Americans were participating enthusiastically in fundraising campaigns organized by the American Red Cross and other humanitarian organizations. Food, clothing, medicine, construction material, and even 7 to 10 million books supplied by public libraries around the country were shipped to Europe. This photograph of a warehouse in the Batignolles station in Paris, packed with crates from the American Relief Clearing House (2), was used for humanitarian purposes to showcase the generosity of the American people. The packages were sorted, prior to distribution by armies of volunteers, in warehouses run by the American Red Cross, like this one in the city of Nancy (1).

2

1-2

Created by Anne Morgan, the American Committee for Devastated France (often known by its French acronym, CARD) sent more than 300 volunteers to Picardy between 1917 and 1924 to help French refugees. It worked hard to promote the actions of the American humanitarian organization, which was largely dependent on the generosity of its donors. On the wall behind this portrait of Anne Morgan with French Prime Minister Aristide Briand are posters used for fundraising campaigns for the reconstruction of northern France (1). With most men mobilized or killed in combat, French women were central to the messages disseminated by philanthropic institutions: several are depicted in the poster on the right, working the land and breastfeeding. The poster on the left shows a seated elderly man holding a child in his arms. In another photograph, Anne Morgan is talking with a group of children in one of the devastated regions (2). Images of children as war victims became widespread in humanitarian photographs. It was for this young generation that soldiers fought, in the hope of building a world free of war. CARD, too, was working to reconstruct France for these children.

A FAREWELL TO ARMS

In the night of November 7 to 8, 1918, a group of German emissaries appeared along the French lines at La Capelle, a town in the Aisne *département*. A white flag was flying from the back of the first car. The delegation, led by Matthias Erzberger, Secretary of State without a portfolio in Max von Baden's government, had come to discuss the conditions of the armistice. After a final identity check, the Germans headed back across regions devastated by fighting. Several hours later, they reached a clearing in the Forest of Compiègne, near the Rethondes train station, where talks were held with Marshall Foch. An Associated Press correspondent saw them drive by and sent a telegram to his New York office: "PARIS URGENT ARMISTICE ALLIES GERMANY SIGNED ELEVEN [THI]SMORNING HOSTILITIES CEASED TWO [THIS]AFTERNOON SEDAN TAKEN [THIS]MORNING BY AMERICANS." Several East Coast newspapers printed special editions with headlines announcing the end of the war. It wasn't until late that afternoon that the State Department published an embarrassed press release refuting the news. The momentary enthusiasm transformed into anger. The police had to intervene to disperse demonstrators who were burning newspapers in the streets.[1]

This story of a fake armistice exemplified the overall mood in the United States several days before November 11, 1918: a combination of feverish enthusiasm and uncertainty toward the long-awaited end of fighting on the Western Front. During the entire month of October, Germans and Americans had exchanged diplomatic notes to clarify the provisions of the peace offer. "During the armistice, we did not know the exact state of the German forces, and we accepted it with the idea that the following day it could no longer be possible," Clemenceau would later admit. "If we had had better information, we would have imposed more severe conditions." In reality, it was President Wilson who led the negotiations with the enemy, drawing on his famous Fourteen Points Speech of January 8, 1918. He faced opposition from certain members of the American political class who considered that he was being overly complaisant. Massachusetts senator Henry Cabot Lodge, for example, who had already opposed the neutrality policy

American soldiers in the 64th regiment of the 7th Infantry Division celebrate the news of the armistice on the morning of November 11, yet victorious armies were also armies in mourning. The 7th Division, for example, lost more than 1,700 men in the last month of fighting in the Meuse *département*.

1

adopted by the American government in 1914, believed that the Allies should wait until they invaded Germany to demand an unconditional surrender. President Raymond Poincaré of France agreed with this assessment; he blamed the armistice for stopping the successful momentum of the Allied troops and for "hamstringing" French soldiers. But every extra day of fighting also resulted in additional losses. "Our troops are weary," Clemenceau admitted.

The U.S. Army, which expected the conflict to continue through at least 1919 or 1920, did not have any demobilization plan in place. In the fall of 1918, 1.5 million men were still in training in America. Two hundred fifty thousand citizens had just been drafted. They would all be home by February 1919. The real problem concerned the 2 million soldiers, more or less, who had already sailed across the Atlantic. While ships were commissioned to bring them back to America, the soldiers had to wait. In this period, halfway between war and peace, boredom became the primary enemy. Military training alternated with distractions, such as sports activities and theater performances, organized by the YMCA. The Château de Versailles, the Hôtel des Invalides, and Lafayette's tomb attracted many tourists, who set out to discover "la Belle France." "The city of Nice is full of Americans," noted a shopkeeper who was delighted that the Promenade had been invaded by soldiers on leave. In 1919, the Sorbonne offered its first "Cours de Civilisation Française" geared to the doughboys. At the same time, 200,000 American soldiers were sent to the region around Koblenz as an occupying force. German villages had been untouched by the war and, compared to the French countryside, seemed clean and modern to the Americans. In letters, the U.S. soldiers were careful to distinguish between the German people, whom they found welcoming, and the autocratic regimes that had led Germany to its downfall. In contrast, they were filled with reproach for the ingratitude of the French. Some letters were so vehement they worried the military staff. "We fought on the wrong side," wrote certain soldiers. On June 28, 1919, the same day on which the Treaty of Versailles was signed, a riot broke out in the city of Brest, to shouts of "The war is over, Americans get out now!"[2]

When they returned to the United States, most of the demobilized soldiers transited through the port of Hoboken, then boarded trains to take them home. In the first six months of 1919, more than 500 parades were organized across the country. These first local demonstrations commemorating the Great War were marked by the relentless shadow of death, as the memory of the losses was combined with

1-2-3
On November 11, 1918, special newspaper editions headlined the signing of the armistice (1). Civilians wave them in front of the camera, as if to corroborate the news. After months of heavy fighting, the announcement, even though expected, still seemed somewhat unreal. One month later, on December 18, the first American regiments returning from France landed in Hoboken, New Jersey. From there, they were transported by ferry to Long Island, then to Camp Mills, where they were officially discharged (2). Of all the demobilization rituals, the return of weapons (3), here at Camp Dix, in New Jersey, was symbolically one of the most meaningful. Handing in one's weapon meant that these men were no longer soldiers, and accepted a return to peacetime norms.

the celebration of the victorious troops. On September 10, 1919, thousands of wounded from the 1st Infantry Division, the last fighting unit to return to America from the Western Front, participated in the four-hour-long parade down Fifth Avenue, from 107th Street to Washington Square. Cavalrymen led the troops, carrying banners indicating their losses: "First Division, killed: 4,964. Wounded: 17,201." But with the exception of New York and Washington, D.C., which gave a triumphant welcome to General Pershing in the fall of 1919, the rest of the country had already started to leave the war behind. The last soldiers to be demobilized felt almost as if they were intruders. "By the time Krebs returned to his home town in Oklahoma the greeting of heroes was over," wrote Hemingway, in his short story *Soldier's Home*. "He came back much too late. The men from the town who had been drafted had all been welcomed elaborately on their return. There had been a great deal of hysteria. Now the reaction had set in. People seemed to think it was rather ridiculous for Krebs to be getting back so late, years after the war was over."[3]

2

Not all of the American infantrymen fought along the Western Front. The 332nd Infantry Regiment served in Italy, where it participated in the Battle of Vittorio Veneto in late October and early November 1918. After being stationed in Austria and on the Dalmatian coast, these men returned to the United States in mid-April 1919. In the fall of 1918, several thousand American soldiers, most of them from Michigan, were part of an international contingent deployed to the Arkhangelsk region of northern Russia, while the country was in the midst of a civil war. It was known as the Polar Bear Expedition, for the brutal conditions endured by the soldiers, who were not repatriated until July 1919. Finally, the 27th and 31st Infantry Regiments, arriving from the Philippines, joined the coalition that landed in Vladivostok in September 1918 to hold the Trans-Siberian Railway and provide support to the Czech Legion allies. After trying, unsuccessfully, to maintain a neutral stance, given the extremely violent situation that opposed the Bolshevik troops and the counterrevolutionary forces of Admiral Alexander Kolchak, the American Expeditionary Force commanded by General William S. Graves withdrew from Siberia between January 26 and April 1, 1920.

3

After returning home from war, every doughboy received a 60-dollar bonus, a uniform, a coat, a pair of shoes, and, if he had served in Europe, his helmet and a gas mask as souvenirs—meager compensation given the problems they faced in the United States. The Department of War had promised that no veteran would be considered to

4

be demobilized until he had found a job. Some companies, like Ford, reserved jobs for vets. The 240,000 war-wounded received support to re-enter the work force. But during the six months following the armistice, the end of contracts with the war industries resulted in the loss of nearly 360,000 jobs, notably in weapons, naval shipyards, and the textile and metal industries. The impact of the postwar recession hit the northeast region particularly hard, as it also had to handle the largest number of returning soldiers. "I know that we were all crying to go home," confessed one of them. "But now that we're here, I have to admit that I feel a bit lost and strangely alone. Our United States looks really artificial and empty to me."[4]

Disillusionment was widespread among both veterans and diplomats. Influenced by the Calvinist ethics of individualism and the community, the American president defended the idea of a fair peace, based on a sort of covenant that would end not only the Great War, but war itself, forever. "For a brief moment, Wilson stopped being an ordinary politician; he became a messiah," summed up British author H.G. Wells. The aftermath of the war would be marked by the failure of Wilsonian diplomacy as a basis for reforging international relations.[5] The diplomatic defeat paralleled a political defeat. On March 19, 1920, the U.S. Senate refused to ratify the Treaty of Versailles. The legacy of the Great War have had an enduring impact on the foreign policy of the United States, a country torn between isolationism and an awareness of its unique responsibility in a globalized world.

4
French Prime Minister Georges Clemenceau (left), American President Woodrow Wilson (center), and British Prime Minister David Lloyd George (right) after signing the peace treaty in the Hall of Mirrors at the Château de Versailles, on June 28, 1919.

5
On November 11, 1918, a massive crowd filled Broad Street, in Philadelphia. A gigantic replica of the Statue of Liberty had been erected on April 6 to coincide with the launch of the Third Liberty Loan. When the armistice was announced, the city's residents flocked to this symbolic site, even though at that time, an invisible threat should have discouraged this type of demonstration: since the month of March, the Spanish flu pandemic had hit every region of the country.

1 David M. Kennedy, Over Here: The First World War and American Society, op. cit., pp. 231–32. 2 Jennifer D. Keene, Doughboys, the Great War and the Remaking of America, Baltimore and London, The Johns Hopkins University Press, 2001, p. 125. 3 Ernest Hemingway, Soldier's Home, New York, Charles Scribner's Sons, 1925. 4 Dixon Wecter, When Johnny Comes Marching Home, Boston, Houghton Mifflin, 1944, p. 320. 5 Leonard V. Smith, "Les États-Unis et l'échec d'une seconde mobilisation," in Stéphane Audoin-Rouzeau and Christophe Prochasson, eds., Sortir de la Grande Guerre : le monde et l'après-1918, Paris, Tallandier, 2008, pp. 69–91.

5

1

1
A crowd, primarily consisting of young
men, waves American flags in a street in
Chicago, on November 11, 1918.

2
In a village recaptured from the
Germans, near Saint-Mihiel, a group of
soldiers renamed a street "Wilson USA"
after the armistice was declared. They
were not alone in linking the 1918
victory to the name of the American
president. All over the world, Woodrow
Wilson had become a symbol of
postwar aspirations: a new type of
diplomacy, based on collective security,
the creation of international
organizations like the League of
Nations, and the right to self-
determination. Soon, however, the
Wilsonian dream would be replaced by
disillusionment in Europe and in the
colonies. What the historian Erez
Manela called the "Wilsonian moment"
would only last a few months.

2

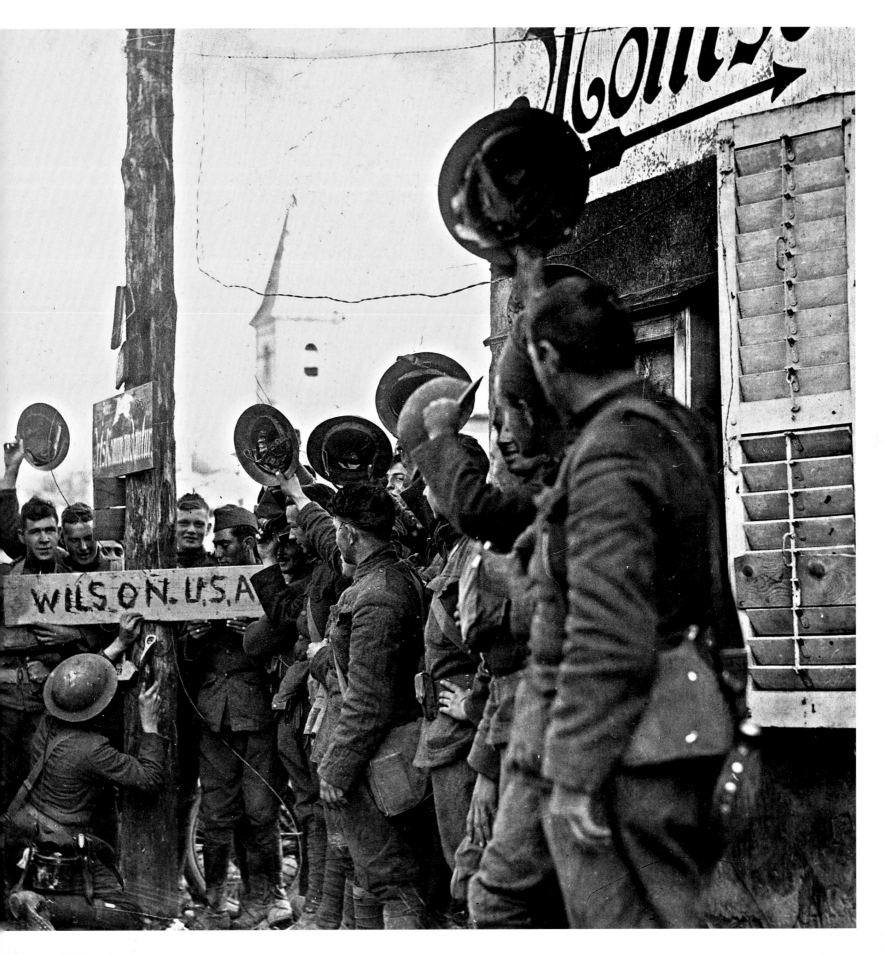

1

1-2
In the immediate aftermath of World War I, President Woodrow Wilson embodied collective hopes for a profound change in international relations. Wilson was the first American president to travel to Europe while in office, for the peace conference. Upon Wilson's arrival in France on December 13, 1919, the mayor of Brest greeted him as "the Apostle of Liberty," who came to liberate the European peoples from their sufferings. This exceptional popularity was reflected in banners hung up in Paris for his arrival, like this one on Rue Royale, in mid-December 1918 (1). In the United States, Wilson's cult status could be seen as an expression of patriotism in a country at war. In this famous photograph by Arthur Mole, 21,000 soldiers in Camp Sherman, Ohio, formed a living portrait of the American president (2).

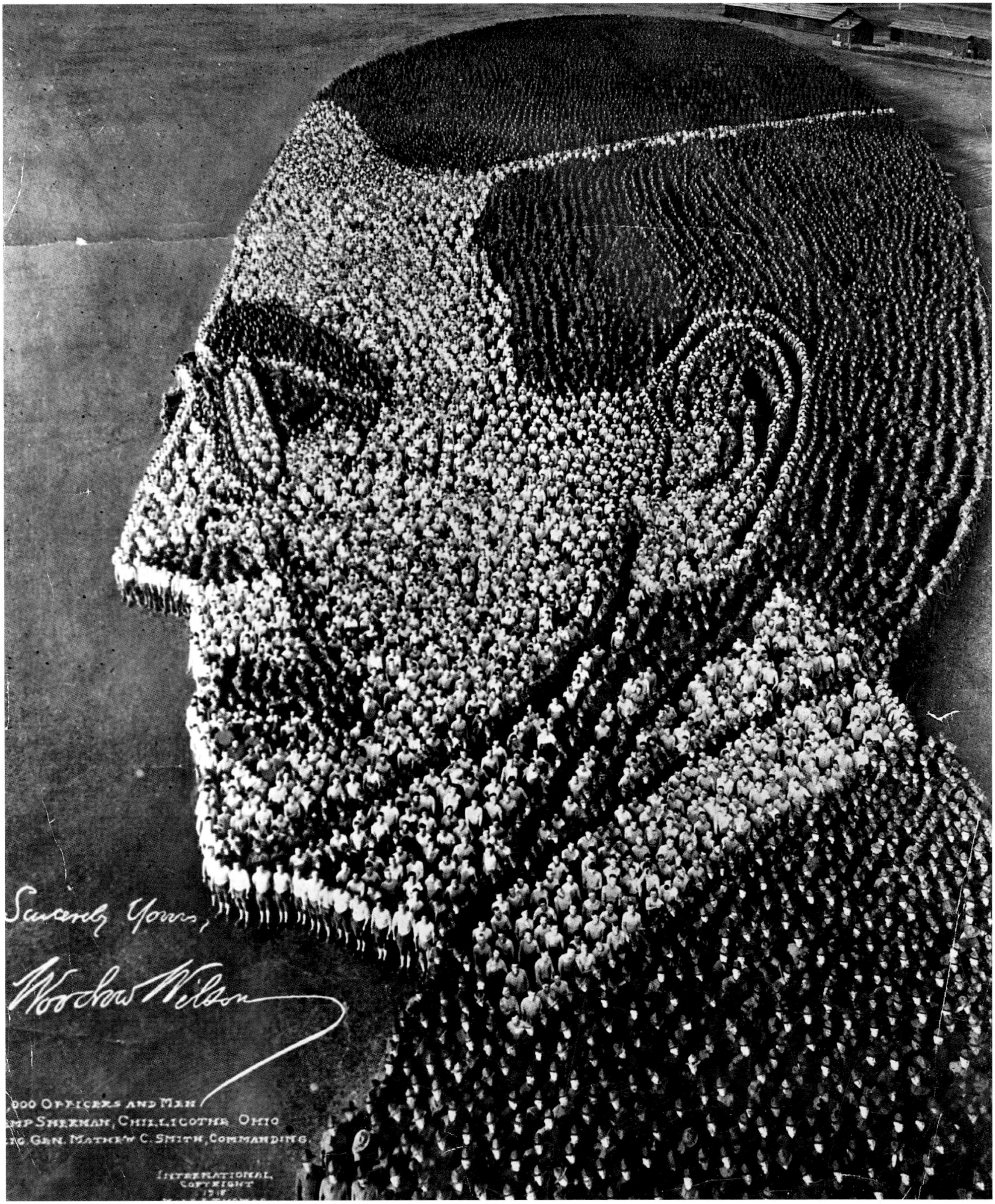

Sincerely Yours,
Woodrow Wilson
000 OFFICERS AND MEN
MP SHERMAN, CHILLICOTHE OHIO
G. GEN. MATHEW C. SMITH, COMMANDING.
INTERNATIONAL
COPYRIGHT

To commemorate the signing of the Treaty of Versailles, France decided to organize an unprecedented parade on July 14, 1919. "An epic parade," headlined a French daily newspaper, stretching nearly six miles, from the bridge in Neuilly to Place de la République. A cenotaph was placed under the Arc de Triomphe. One thousand disabled veterans opened the procession, followed by delegations from all the Allied armies. The number of regiments passing through Place de la Concorde was spectacular, but for millions of survivors, collective mourning outweighed the joy of victory.

Every demobilization is a journey, with its own phases, rhythms, and rituals. After a two-week Atlantic crossing, the soldiers finally caught a glimpse of New York and the iconic silhouettes of skyscrapers. The Manhattan skyline, so different from those of the Old Continent, offered a distinctive backdrop to those returning from war. For local regiments, like the 369th Infantry, this cityscape meant an imminent reunion with family and friends. But most of the demobilized soldiers still faced several days of travel before they would finally reach home.

1

At the entrance to the port of Hoboken, the upper deck of the USS *Agamemnon* was filled with soldiers admiring the breathtaking view of New York City. This transatlantic passenger ship, constructed by the Germans in the Stettin shipyards, was named SS *Kaiser Wilhelm II* before the war. Seized by the American government in April 1917, it was used as a barracks ship, then as transport taking troops to the European front starting in late October 1917. In early 1919, it made nine successive trips between France and the United States, bringing more than 40,000 American soldiers back home.

2

Men from the 369th Infantry Regiment just before landing in New York. The Harlem Hellfighters, commanded by Colonel William Hayward, had spent six months in combat duty, more than any other unit in the U.S. Army. The unit was awarded the French Croix de Guerre for its exceptional performance at Château-Thierry and at Belleau Wood.

1

1-2

In March 1919, newly discharged
soldiers savor the tart taste and
cinnamon smell of apple pies—
this traditional American dish is far
more than just any old dessert (1).
After the traumatic experience of
combat and mass death, the veterans
wanted to rediscover the reassuring
flavors of prewar existence.
Young fathers proudly hold their
children in this photograph (2), a simple
gesture marking the return to family
life after the war. It was also a way to
demonstrate that family bonds
remained strong after months apart,
and that it was time to look toward the
future that was represented by a new
generation.

2

1-2

Parades were one of the most significant rituals surrounding the return of the soldiers (1). The processions told the story of the Great War, by honoring one or another regiment and paying tribute to the dead and the wounded. The mayor of New York launched a fundraising campaign to finance three monuments to be placed along Fifth Avenue, photographed here at the New York Public Library (2). They included the Arch of Jewels, decorated with crystal and lit up at night; the Court of the Dead, with the names of the battles in which the U.S. Army participated; and the Arch of Victory, depicting allegorical figures of Democracy and Justice, on 24th Street—marking the passage of the troops through the city.

2

1

1-2
Returning soldiers welcomed every sign
of recognition, from the most
spectacular to the humblest. The
parades, even when they were
organized locally, as here in Harlem (2),
showed them that they had not been
forgotten. An object as seemingly
ordinary as the helmets offered to all
veterans had significant symbolic value.
After the parade down Fifth Avenue, the
black soldiers of the 369th Infantry
Regiment received a pack of cigarettes
during the dinner served in their honor
(1). In a deeply segregated country, this
gesture of gratitude was no small thing.

African-American women and children lining Fifth Avenue to watch the men of the 369th Infantry Regiment pass by, on February 21, 1919. When they left for the front, in December 1917, the Harlem Hellfighters had not been allowed to participate in the farewell parade for the New York National Guard (the Rainbow Division) on the grounds that "black is not a color of the rainbow." Fourteen months later, segregation was as rampant as ever, but Colonel Hayward did everything in his power so that his men would be given a reception worthy of their sacrifice. The veterans of the 369th paraded to the sounds of James Reese Europe's famous jazz band.

1-2

A wounded African-American soldier, with an amputated leg, is greeted by the crowd during the parade of the 369th Regiment (1). For centuries, the war-wounded and disabled had been reduced to poverty and begging. World War I represented a major turning point, with recognition of the rights of war victims, supported by veteran associations. Care for the wounded varied depending on the country, and in the United States, on race. That said, wartime medicine, reconstructive surgery, and the manufacture of prosthetic devices made significant progress from 1914 to 1918 and in the 1920s. This photograph, taken in early 1919 at Walter Reed Hospital, in Washington, D.C. (2), shows wounded soldiers knitting. A feminine gendered activity, knitting was used to reduce the severity of tremors for soldiers suffering from shell shock. The war led to a crisis of masculinity. Disabled veterans often felt emasculated, a shadow of their former selves.

1

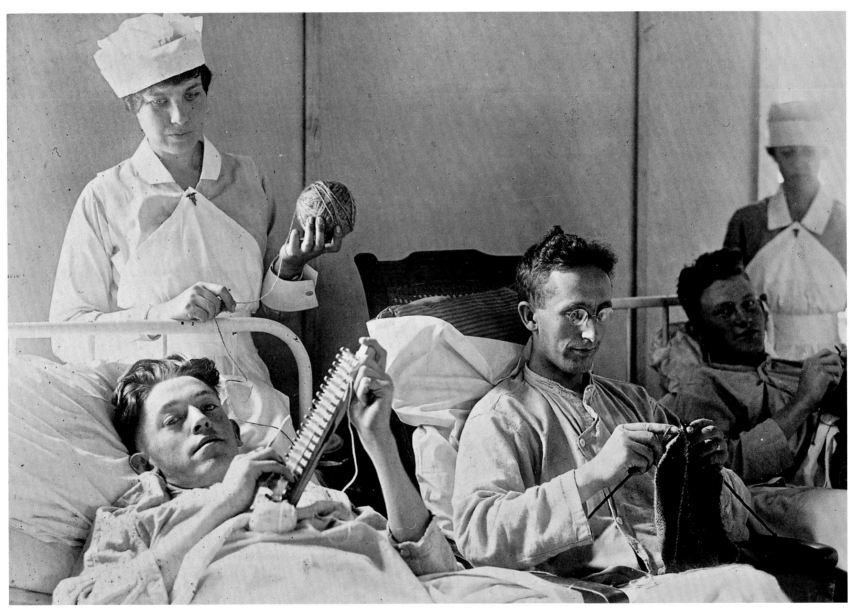

2

1

2

With a considerable number of killed and missing, the Great War posed unprecedented challenges. Should the tradition of returning the bodies of American soldiers to the families, firmly established since the Spanish-American War of 1898, be maintained? Or leave the deceased on European soil, with their fellow soldiers, as called for by General Pershing and Theodore Roosevelt, who lost his son Quentin in aerial combat in the summer of 1918? Ultimately, the decision whether or not to repatriate the bodies was left to the families. By April 1921, the American Graves Registration Service had collected the remains of 14,000 soldiers (2), then returned them to the United States (1). For certain families, this was a significant step in their grieving process.

Three mothers of soldiers killed in battle and three familiar faces of grief, an image that deeply affected the American population. During the war, military families added a blue star to the flags flying on their homes. When a soldier died in combat, the blue star was replaced by a gold star. In the period between the two World Wars, the Gold Star Mothers, as they are called, had access to government-financed programs to make pilgrimages to the battlefields. While American soldiers were buried in the same military cemeteries, irrespective of race, white and black mothers traveled aboard separate ships and did not receive the same reception on arrival. Only a few hundred African-American mothers and widows would make the trip to France.

LIST OF ILLUSTRATIONS AND PHOTO CREDITS

FRONT COVER

American soldiers. Saint-Nazaire (Loire-Inférieure), June 26, 1917. Photo Daniau. SPA 1 AD 37/SPCA/ECPAD. Glass plate negative 9 × 12 black and white.

BACK COVER

(1) Men of the 1st Infantry Division on the docks, after landing in France. Saint-Nazaire (Loire-Inférieure) June 26, 1917. Photo Daniau. SPA 1 AD 18/SPCA/ECPAD. Glass plate negative 9 × 12 black and white.

(2) American soldier in a camp in France, ca. 1917. © Universal History Archive/UIG via Getty Images.

(3) A cloud of gas floats toward a trench held by Americans, October 23, 1918. © Underwood & Underwood, New York.

(4) In Chicago, a crowd of young men celebrate the armistice, November 11, 1918. © Chicago History Museum/Getty Images.

INSIDE COVER

Front. Soldiers of the 27th Infantry Division of New York's National Guard, marching to the training camp. September 1917. © Interim Archives/Archives photos/Getty Images.

Back. American troops and colors marching down the Champs-Élysées during the Victory parade, July 14, 1919. © PhotoQuest/Getty Images.

AMERICA'S FORGOTTEN WAR

p. 6 American soldiers (detail). Saint-Nazaire (Loire-Inférieure), June 26, 1917. Photo Daniau. SPA 1 AD 37/SPCA/ECPAD. Glass plate negative 9 × 12 black and white.

p. 11 (1). "Keep these off the U.S.A." Poster for Liberty Bonds. Illustration by John Norton, ca. 1917. © David Pollack/Corbis Historical/Corbis via Getty Images.

p. 11 (2). "Destroy this mad brute. Enlist." Recruitment poster for the U.S. Army. © De Agostini Picture Library/Getty Images.

p. 11 (3). "On Which Side of the Window are YOU?" Recruitment poster for the U.S. Army, 1917. © Universal History Archive/UIG via Getty Images.

I WANT YOU FOR THE U.S. ARMY!

p. 14 Illustrator James Montgomery Flagg posing next to his famous recruitment poster, 1917. © Corbis/Corbis Historical Corbis via Getty Images.

p. 16 (1). *Yale Daily News* staff members pose in their uniforms after enlisting. ca. 1918. © FPG/Hulton Archives/Getty Images.

p. 17 (2). Medical exam for young recruits. New York, ca. 1917. © FPG/Hulton Archives/Getty Images.

p. 17 (3). Army recruiter administering an IQ test to a black soldier, March 1918. © Bettmann/Getty Images.

p. 18 (1). Obstacle course at Camp Wadsworth, South Carolina, ca. 1918. © National Archives and Records Administration, Washington.

p. 19 (2). Before leaving for the front, the men of the 312th Infantry Regiment parade down the main street of their city, Newark, New Jersey. © National Archives and Records Administration, Washington.

pp. 20–21. The lottery for the first group of draftees called to serve. The blindfolded man is Secretary of War Newton D. Baker. Washington DC, July 20, 1917. © Bettmann/Getty Images.

p. 22 (1). A group of U.S. Marines. Recruitment photograph, 1918. © National Archives and Records Administration, Washington.

p. 23 (2). Three women enlisting in the Marine Corps at Martial Corner of Boston Common, in Boston, Massachusetts, 1917. © Bettmann/Getty Images.

p. 23 (3). Men signing up at a Marine Corps recruitment office. New York, ca. 1917. © Library of Congress/Corbis/VCG via Getty Images.

p. 24 (1). American soldiers aboard a train say goodbye to their families before leaving for the European front, ca. 1917. © Time Life Pictures/National Archives/Getty Images.

p. 24 (2). A final kiss for Private Loughlin of the 69th Infantry Regiment, New York National Guard, 1917. © Interim Archives/Getty Images.

p. 24 (3). A mother escorting her son to the train bound for boot camp, 1917 © Time Life Pictures/Mayor's Office-Newark War Department/National Archives/Time Life Pictures/Getty Images.

p. 25 (4). Mobilization in the United States: recruits in a New York train station, 1917 © Ullstein Bild/Ullstein Bild via Getty Images.

p. 26 (1). Infantrymen training with bayonets, 1917 © Archive Photos/Getty Images.

p. 27 (2). Troops embarking for Europe, ca. 1917. © Anthony Butera/Getty Images.

OVER THERE

p. 28. Landing of American troops. Saint-Nazaire (Loire-Inférieure), June 26, 1917. Photo Daniau. SPA 1 AD 18/SPCA/ECPAD. Glass plate negative 9 × 12 black and white.

p. 30 (1). "American at the front and American at the back" (original caption). France, British headquarters, June 26, 1917. Unknown photographer. SPA 5 RF 20/SPCA/ECPAD. Glass plate negative 12 × 16 black and white.

p. 31 (2). Poster for residents. Saint-Nazaire (Loire-Inférieure), June 29, 1917. Photo Daniau. SPA 1 AD 61/SPCA/ECPAD. Glass plate negative 9 × 12 black and white.

p. 32 (3). Arrival of General Pershing: people crowding around the cars. Paris, Place de la Concorde, June 13, 1917. Photo Bauche. SPA 15 CB 168/SPCA/ECPAD. Glass plate negative 11 × 15 black and white.

p. 33 (4). General Pershing greets the crowd. Paris, Hôtel Crillon, June 13, 1917. Photo Bauche. SPA 15 CB 171/SPCA/ECPAD. Glass plate negative 11 × 15 black and white.

p. 34 (1). Breton woman and American sailor. Brest (Finistère), on the docks, September 25, 1918. Photo Edmond Famechon. SPA 152 R 5164/SPCG/ECPAD. Glass plate negative 6 × 13 stereoscopic black and white (right view).

p. 35 (2). Commercial harbor: fishing boats. Brest (Finistère), September 25, 1918. Photo Edmond Famechon. SPA 152 R 5208/SPCG/ECPAD. Glass plate negative 6 × 13 stereoscopic black and white.

pp. 36–37. American soldiers. Saint-Nazaire (Loire-Inférieure), June 26, 1917. Photo Daniau. SPA 1 AD 37/SPCA/ECPAD. Glass plate negative 9 × 12 black and white.

pp. 38–39 (1). Landing of American troops: transport ship *Havana* and the crowd. Saint-Nazaire (Loire-Inférieure), June 26, 1917. SPA 1 AD 6/SPCA/ECPAD. Glass plate negative 9 × 12 black and white.

p. 39 (2). Unloading the supply ship *Neptune*. Saint-Nazaire (Loire-Inférieure), June 26, 1917. SPA 1 AD 39/SPCA/ECPAD. Glass plate negative 9 × 12 black and white.

pp. 40–41. General Pershing arrives at the station. Saint-Nazaire (Loire-Inférieure), June 26, 1917. Photo Daniau. SPA 1 AD 60/SPCA/ECPAD. Glass plate negative 9 × 12 black and white.

p. 42 (1). American camp at Villès-Martin: U.S. infantrymen knapsacks. Saint-Nazaire (Loire-Inférieure), July 1917. Photo Louis Well. SPA 41 O 1471/SPCA/ECPAD. Glass plate negative 9 × 12 black and white.

p. 43 (2). American camp at Villès-Martin: equipment demonstration. Saint-Nazaire (Loire-Inférieure), July 1917. Photo Louis Well. SPA 43 O 1511/SPCA/ECPAD. Glass plate negative 9 × 12 black and white.

p. 43 (3). Americans at military camp. Near Saint-Nazaire (Loire-Inférieure), June 29, 1917. Photo Daniau. SPA 1 AD 63/SPCA/ECPAD. Glass plate negative 9 × 12 black and white.

p. 44 (1). General Pershing touring the aviation camp with General Dubail; Captain Monteno, head of anti-aircraft defense of the trench camp; and Major Leclerc, squadron commander of the trench camp of Paris. Le Bourget, June 14, 1917. Photo Bauche. SPA 15 CB 194/SPCA/ECPAD. Glass plate negative 11 × 15 black and white.

p. 45 (2). Arrival of American troops: General Pershing giving a speech. Paris, Picpus Cemetery, July 4, 1917. Photo Paul Queste. SPA 104 B 5740/SPCA/ECPAD. Glass plate negative 6 × 13 stereoscopic black and white (left view).

p. 46 (1). Independence Day celebrations: American military parade. Paris, Place d'Iéna, July 4, 1918. Photo Albert Moreau. SPA 311 M 5375/SPCA/ECPAD. Glass plate negative 9 × 12 black and white.

p. 47 (2). Local school: Franco-American celebration. Paris, Rue Riquet, July 4, 1917. Photo Paul Queste. SPA 104 B 5762/SPCA/ECPAD. Glass plate negative 13 × 18 black and white.

THE POLITICS OF RACE

p. 48. African-American volunteers ready to enlist in the 8th Infantry Regiment, in Chicago, Illinois, 1917. © National Archives and Records Administration, Washington.

p. 50 (1). Ike Sims from Atlanta (Georgia), 87 years old, had eleven sons serving in the military, ca. 1917. © National Archives and Records Administration, Washington.

p. 51 (2). A school for African-American soldiers in the 35th Infantry Division in Commercy (Meuse), in France. © Bettmann/Getty Images.

p. 52 (1). The first recruits arrive in Camp Upton on Long Island, New York, September 1917. © National Archives and Records Administration, Washington.

p. 53 (2). Court-martial of 64 African-American soldiers from the 24th Infantry Regiment who participated in the Houston Riot, August 23, 1917. © War Department/Buyenlarge/Getty Images.

p. 54 (1). The jazz band of the 369th Infantry Regiment (formerly the 15th Regiment of the New York National Guard) returning to New York, with band leader Lieutenant James Reese Europe, December 2, 1919. © National Archives and Records Administration, Washington.

p. 55 (2). Lieutenant James Reese Europe, a celebrity on the New York jazz scene, returning from the front with the 369th Infantry Regiment. December 2, 1919. © National Archives and Records Administration, Washington.

p. 56 (1). A soldier entertains his friends with a roller-skate dance. 1918. © National Archives and Records Administration, Washington.

p. 57 (2). African-American soldiers playing checkers. Villers-le-Sec (Marne), April 12, 1918. Photo Auguste Goulden. SPA 24 GO 1129/SPCA/ECPAD. Glass plate negative 8 × 16 stereoscopic black and white.

pp. 58–59. American camp, blacks from the South: a boxing match (original caption). Rembercourt (Meuse), May 31, 1918. Photo Maurice Boulay. SPA 39 BO 1859/SPCA/ECPAD. Glass plate negative 6 × 13 black and white.

p. 60 (1). French and American guards where the two sectors meet up. Avocourt (Meuse), July 19, 1918. Photo Maurice Boulay. SPA 47 BO 2117/SPCA/ECPAD. Glass plate negative 6 × 13 stereoscopic black and white (left view).

p. 61 (2). Black American soldier in front of a dugout (original caption). Avocourt (Meuse), July 19, 1918. Photo Maurice Boulay. SPA 47 BO 2110/SPCA/ECPAD. Glass plate negative 6 × 13 stereoscopic black and white (left view).

INITIATION

p. 62. American infantrymen taking a break. Saint-Clément (Meurthe-et-Moselle), March 22, 1918. Photo Jacques Ridel. SPA 36 W 1814/SPCA/ECPAD. Glass plate negative 6 × 13 stereoscopic black and white (right view).

p. 64 (1). American camp of Villès-Martin: a Franco-American film and photographic crew. Saint-Nazaire (Loire-Inférieure), July 1, 1917. Photo Louis Well. SPA 41 O 1483/SPCA/ECPAD. Glass plate negative 9 × 12 black and white.

p. 65 (2). American escadrille [N 124]: American pilots. Luxeuil (Haute-Saône), May 14, 1916. Photo Gabriel Boussuge. SPA 20 P 244/SPA/ECPAD. Glass plate negative 9 × 12 black and white.

p. 66 (3). American ambulance unit AU-2, evacuating a wounded soldier. Récourt (Meuse), August 15, 1916. Photo Pierre Machard. SPA 27 C 2625/SPCA/ECPAD. Glass plate negative 13 × 18 black and white.

p. 66 (4). African-Americans burying a fellow soldier on the front. © US Army Signal Corps/The Life Picture collection/Getty Images.

p. 67 (5). American tanks advance in support of French troops to recapture the village of Juvigny, near Soissons, October 26, 1918. © Underwood & Underwood, New York

p. 68 (1). American Army (1st Roosevelt Battalion): training field, digging a trench. Demange (Meuse), August 20, 1917. Photo Auguste Goulden. SPA 9 GO 454/SPCA/ECPAD. Glass plate negative 9 × 12 black and white.

p. 69 (2). Grenade launch training center at the American camp: an American soldier is cheered by his comrades after successfully launching a grenade. Mauvages (Meuse), July 27, 1917. Photo Albert Samama-Chikli. SPA 57 L 2666/SPCA/domaine public/collections ECPAD. Glass plate negative 6 × 13 stereoscopic black and white.

p. 70 (1). American camp: French and Americans explain how to use their respective rifles. Houdelaincourt (Meuse), July 26, 1917. Photo Albert Moreau. SPA 211 M 4188/SPCA/ECPAD. Glass plate negative 9 × 12 black and white.

p. 70 (2). Rest camp for the U.S. 109th Infantry Regiment. Louppy-le-Château (Meuse), September 14, 1918. Photo Lavergne. SPA 329 M 5554/SPCG/ECPAD. Glass plate negative 9 × 12 black and white.

p. 71 (3). American camp: U.S. soldiers and French instructors. Tréveray (Meuse), July 28, 1917. Photo Albert Samama-Chikli. SPA 57 L 2679/SPCA/domaine public/collections ECPAD. Glass plate negative 6 × 13 stereoscopic black and white.

p. 72 (1). American soldier wearing a gas mask, March 9, 1918. © National Archives and Records Administration, Washington.

p. 72 (2). Sergeant Joseph Levin of the Chemical Warfare Service. He and his horse are both fitted with gas masks, ca. 1917. © Hirz/Archive Photos/Getty Images.

p. 73 (3). American camp: testing gas masks. Dommiers (Aisne), June 2, 1917. Photo Emmanuel Mas. SPA 77 S 3288/SPCA/ECPAD. Glass plate negative 9 × 12 black and white.

pp. 74–75. American cavalry riding through a village. Crézancy (Aisne), July 17, 1918. Photo Maurice Boulay. SPA 47 BO 2092/SPCA/ECPAD.Glass plate negative 6 × 13 black and white.

p. 76 (1). American artillery: loading a 203-mm Howitzer. Senoncourt (Meuse), July 17, 1918. Photo Maurice Boulay. SPA 47 BO 2101/SPCA/ECPAD. Glass plate negative 6 × 13 black and white.

p. 77 (2). American artillery: aiming a 203-mm Howitzer. Senoncourt (Meuse), July 17, 1918. Photo Maurice Boulay. SPA 47 BO 2102/SPCA/ECPAD. Glass plate negative 13 × 18 black and white.

p. 78 (1). American soldiers manning a machine gun in the second line trench in Dieffmatten, Alsace, June 26, 1918. © Underwood & Underwood, New York.

p. 79. A cloud of gas floats toward a trench held by Americans, October 23, 1918. © Underwood & Underwood, New York.

pp. 80–81. American troops, supported by French tanks, attack and capture Cantigny. Cantigny (Somme), May 28, 1918. Photo Edmond Famechon. SPA 127 R 4522/SPCA/ECPAD. Glass plate negative 6 × 13 stereoscopic black and white.

p. 82 (1). Military preparation societies at tombs of American soldiers: M. Lattès giving a speech. Belleau Wood (Aisne), September 8, 1918. Photo Joly. SPA 67 X 2787/SPCG/ECPAD. Glass plate negative 9 × 12 black and white.

p. 83 (2). Funeral for an American soldier killed in action. © European/FPG/Getty Images.

p. 84 (1). Tomb of pilot and First Lieutenant Quentin Roosevelt. Near Cierges (Aisne). Photo Cordier. SPA 24 G 908/SPCA/ECPAD. Glass plate negative 9 × 12 black and white.

p. 85 (2). Cemetery: tomb of an American ambulance driver. Moosch (Haut-Rhin), September 8, 1916. Photo Paul Dubray. SPA 50 T 1978/SPA/ECPAD. Glass plate negative 9 × 12 black and white.

p. 86 (1). Two American soldiers on the devastated main square. Fismes (Marne), September 11, 1918. Photo Daniau. SPA 13 AD 361/SPCG/ECPAD. Glass plate negative 6 × 13 stereoscopic black and white.

p. 87 (2). Souvenir from Verdun: in Cheppy, Argonne, an African-American soldier in front of signs indicating different locations, including that of the YMCA, 1918. © JHU Sheridan Libraries/Gado/Getty Images.

p. 88 (1). American medical unit camp no. 7. Chassemy (Aisne), September 26, 1917. Photo Maurice Boulay. SPA 21 BO 1261/SPCA/ECPAD. Glass plate negative 6 × 13 stereoscopic black and white.

p. 89 (2). Camp Franklin, training American units: American soldier. Near Naix-aux-Forges (Meuse), August 27, 1917. Photo Albert Moreau. SPA 216 M 4271/SPCA/ECPAD. Glass plate negative 9 × 12 black and white.

p. 90 (1). American camp: soldiers washing their clothes. Tréveray (Meuse), October 1917. Photo Auguste Goulden. SPA 10 GO 559/SPCA/ECPAD. Glass plate negative 9 x 12 black and white.

p. 91 (2). African-American troops bathing. Fresnes-sur-Apance (Haute-Marne), July 20, 1918. Photo Gustave Alaux. SPA 41 IS 1596/SPCA/ECPAD. Glass plate negative 9 × 12 black and white.

p. 92 (1). American camp: group of children and American soldiers. Gondrecourt (Meuse), August 20, 1917. Photo Auguste Goulden. SPA 9 GO 443/SPCA/ECPAD. Glass plate negative 9 × 12 black and white.

p. 93 (2). American camp: Americans drawing water from a well. Gondrecourt (Meuse), July 28, 1917. Photo Ernest Baguet. SPA 40 Y 1838/SPCA/ECPAD. Glass plate negative 9 × 12 black and white.

p. 93 (3). American officers, guests of a local family. Gondrecourt (Meuse), July 27, 1917. Photo Albert Samama-Chikli. SPA 57 L 2661/SPCA/domaine public/collections ECPAD. Glass plate negative 6 × 13 stereoscopic black and white.

pp. 94–95. Americans on leave touring the country. La Chambotte, near Aix-les-Bains (Savoie), April 17, 1918. Photo Paul Queste. SPA 142 B 7092/SPCA/ECPAD. Glass plate negative 9 × 12 black and white.

AMERICANS ALL

p. 96. Ten thousand sailors at the Great Lakes Training Station, Illinois, form a human flag for a propaganda photo, 1918. © PhotoQuest/Getty Images.

p. 98 (1). Manufacturing helmets for soldiers in the plant of the Hale & Kilburn Corporation. New York, 1917. © War Department/Buyenlarge/Getty Images.

p. 99 (2). Women filled in for jobs left vacant as men were sent to the front. Here, a policewoman patrolling her beat in New York. © George Rinhart/Corbis via Getty Images.

p. 100 (3). Airplane leaving the hangar of the Wright plant, Dayton, Ohio. July 25, 1918. © National Archives and Records Administration, Washington.

p. 101 (4). Interior view of the munitions plant, Bethlehem Steel Factory, Bethlehem, Pennsylvania, ca. 1918. © Popperfoto/Getty Images.

p. 102 (1). Ernestine Schumann-Heink, a famous singer, and two veterans participate in a rally to promote Liberty Bonds, 1918. © Bettmann/Getty Images.

p. 103 (2). Mary Pickford with Charlie Chaplin and Douglas Fairbanks. These three film stars headlined an event, the Victory Bond Rally. © Bettmann/Getty Images.

p. 104 (1). A student from Vassar College, a volunteer for farmwork, driving a tractor, October 16, 1917. © Bettmann/Getty Images.

p. 105 (2). A woman contributes to the war effort by working in a munitions factory. © FPG/ Archive Photos/ Getty Images.

p. 106 (1). A police officer fingerprints a European "enemy alien," in New York. © Bettmann/Getty Images.

p. 107 (2). Children in front of an anti-German sign posted in Edison Park. Chicago, 1917. © Chicago History Museum/Getty Images.

p. 108 (1). A New York street sweeper wearing a mask to help check the spread of the Spanish flu, 1918. © PhotoQuest/Archive Photos/Getty Images.

p. 109 (2). Military hospital of Camp Funston (Kansas), emergency facilities during the Spanish flu pandemic, 1918. © Otis Historical Archives National Museum of Health and Medicine.

THE POWER OF HUMANITARIANISM

p. 110. Evacuating a wounded soldier. Westouter (Belgium), May 30, 1918. Photo Marcel Lorée. SPA 14 LO 1163/SPCA/ECPAD. Glass plate negative 9 × 12 black and white.

p. 112 (1). Herbert Hoover (1874–1964), founder of a vast relief program to help French and Belgian civilians under German occupation, and the future 31st president of the United States, poses with his family in front of stacks of thank-you letters. © A.R. Coster/Topical Press Agency/ Getty Images.

p. 113 (2). Grateful Flemish schoolchidren, detail of a photograph on display at the "Remembering Herbert Hoover" exhibition in Brussels, 2006. © Paul O'Driscoll/Bloomberg via Getty Images.

p. 114 (3). Nurses and boy scouts participating in a fundraising campaign in the streets of Birmingham, Alabama, May 1918. © National Archives and Records Administration, Washington.

p. 115 (4). American looking at a destroyed bridge in liberated Château-Thierry (Aisne), July 23, 1918. Photo Maurice Boulay. SPA 44 BO 2000/SPCA/ECPAD. Glass plate negative 6 × 13 stereoscopic black and white (right view).

p. 116 (1). Arrival of wounded French soldiers: the American Red Cross transports them to hospitals. Aix-les-Bains (Savoie), May 1918. Photo Cordier. SPA 23 G 896/SPCA/ECPAD. Glass plate negative 13 × 18 black and white.

p. 117 (2). American ambulance: the California unit prepared to head to the French front. Paris, 21 rue Raynouard, March 19, 1917. Photo Paul Queste. SPA 91 B 5108/SPCA/ECPAD. Glass plate negative 6 × 13 stereoscopic black and white.

p. 118 (1). Students volunteering to become military nurses taking a course at the Vassar College training camp. Poughkeepsie, September 18, 1918. © National Archives and Records Administration, Washington.

p. 119 (2). Hôpital du Grand Palais: bone graft by Dr. Laurent (second and final phase of the operation). Paris, March 17, 1917. Photo Paul Queste. SPA 91 B 5094/SPCA/ECPAD. Glass plate negative 13 × 18 black and white.

p. 120 (1). An American Red Cross warehouse. Nancy (Meurthe-et-Moselle), March 1, 1918. Photo Joly. SPA 62 X 2385/SPCA/ECPAD. Glass plate negative 9 × 12 black and white.

p. 121 (2). The main hall of the train station, with crates containing American donations to the American Relief Clearing House. Paris, Batignolles station, June 21, 1916. Photo Albert Moreau. SPA 98 M 2188/SPA/ECPAD. Glass plate negative 9 × 12 black and white.

p. 122 (1). Aristide Briand and Anne Morgan, President of the American Committee for Devastated France (CARD), New York, 1921. © AgenceRol/Bnf, Paris.

p. 123 (2). Children in devastated regions come to get shoes at the Pierpont-Morgan charity. Blérancourt (Aisne), September 30, 1917. Photo Maurice Grosclaude. SPA 6 OX 106/SPCA/ECPAD. Glass plate negative 8.5 × 10 black and white.

A FAREWELL TO ARMS

p. 124. Soldiers of the 64th Regiment and the 7th Infantry Division celebrate the news of the armistice on the morning of November 11, 1918. © National Archives and Records Administration, Washington.

p. 126 (1). In Washington, jubilant civilians show newspaper headlines announcing Germany's surrender. November 11, 1918. © Bettmann/Getty Images.

p. 127 (2). Heading to their debarkation camp, the first returning soldiers transit through Long Island City. December 18, 1918. © National Archives and Records Administration, Washington.

p. 127 (3). Demobilized soldiers returning their equipment to the Army. November 27, 1918. © National Archives and Records Administration, Washington.

p. 128 (4). Signing the peace treaty: arrival of Prime Ministers Clemenceau and Lloyd George and President Wilson. Versailles, June 28, 1919. Photo Roger Le Baron. SPA 83 A 3101/SPCA/ECPAD. Glass plate negative 6 × 13 stereoscopic black and white.

p. 129 (5). Following the announcement of the armistice, a massive crowd fills the streets on all sides of a replica of the Statue of Liberty on Broad Street, in Philadelphia. © National Archives and Records Administration, Washington.

p. 130 (1). In Chicago, a crowd of young men celebrates the armistice, November 11, 1918. © Chicago History Museum/Archive Photos/Getty Images.

p. 131 (2). In a village recaptured from the Germans, near Saint-Mihiel, Amercan soldiers renamed a street "Wilson U.S.A.," 1918. © PhotoQuest/Archive Photos/Getty Images.

p. 132 (1). President Wilson's visit: the official parade on Rue Royale. Paris, December 14, 1918. Photo Amédée Eywinger. SPA 82 E 3608/SPCG/ECPAD. Glass plate negative 9 × 12 black and white.

p. 133 (2). Twenty-one thousand soldiers form a living portrait of President Wilson at Camp Sherman, Ohio, 1918. © Mole and Thomas/Hulton Archives/Getty Images.

pp. 134–135. Military parade of American troops. Paris, Place de la Concorde, July 14, 1919. Photo Pierre Machard. SPA 69 C 4859/SPCG/ECPAD. Glass plate negative 9 × 12 black and white.

pp. 136–137. A troop transport ship arriving in New York, ca. 1919. © Hulton Picture/Getty Images.

p. 138 (1). Soldiers returning from France cheer from the upper bridge of the USS *Agamemnon* as they enter Hoboken harbor, ca. 1919. © Bettmann/Getty Images.

p. 139 (2). Soldiers of the 369th Infantry Regiment, just before arriving in New York, December 1919. © Bettmann/Getty Images.

p. 140 (1). Infantrymen just home from Europe eat American apple pies, March 14, 1919. © Underwood Archives/Archive Photos/Getty Images.

p. 141 (2). Back with their families, young fathers proudly hold their children, ca. 1919. © Universal History Archive/UIG via Getty Images.

p. 142 (1). A victory parade in 1918. © Time Life Pictures/US Army Signal Corps/Time Life Pictures/Getty Images.

p. 143 (2). A military parade on Fifth Avenue, New York. © Bettmann/Getty Images.

p. 144 (1). After the parade, dinner and cigarettes at the 71st Regiment Armory for the soldiers of the 369th Infantry Regiment. New York, December 17, 1919. © Bettmann/Getty Images.

p. 145 (2). African-American troops parade over the bridge at 145th Street and Lenox Avenue, in Harlem, New York. © Bettmann/Getty Images.

pp. 146–147. African-American children give a triumphant welcome to their fathers in the 369th Regiment, parading on Fifth Avenue. New York, February 21, 1919. © National Archives and Records Administration, Washington.

p. 148 (1). An African-American soldier who lost his leg greets the crowd during the parade of the 369th Infantry Regiment. © Bettmann/Getty Images.

p. 149 (2). War-wounded knitting at Walter Reed Hospital. Washington, ca. 1919. © National Archives and Records Administration, Washington.

p. 150 (1). Religious services in Hoboken for 1,609 soldiers who died in France, March 16, 1921. © FPG/Hulton Archives/Getty Images.

p. 151 (2). Coffins of American soldiers who died in action transit through a warehouse in Antwerp, Belgium, ca. 1918. © FPG/Hulton Archives/Getty Images.

pp. 152–153. *Goodwill Delegation.* Three Gold Star Mothers set sail for France as goodwill ambassadors, ca. 1918. © FPG/Hulton Archives/Getty Images.

The DMPA

La Direction de la Mémoire, du Patrimoine et des Archives (DMPA, Directorate of Remembrance, Heritage and Archives) is a unit of the French Ministry of Defense, acting under the authority of the Secretary General of the ministry. The DMPA has particular responsibility for the ministry's cultural policy through the collections of its museums, archives, and libraries. It decides on and funds the necessary initiatives for managing and promoting this rich legacy. As part of this mission, the DMPA also publishes and provides support for the production of books and audiovisual materials, allowing the general public to discover the history and heritage of the Ministry of Defense.

The ECPAD

The Établissement de Communication et de Production Audiovisuelle de la Défense (ECPAD, French Defense audiovisual agency) is a French Ministry of Defense department that oversees audiovisual coverage. Its military reporters participate in every theater of operations, in France and around the world. Tasked with recording major Ministry of Defense events, the ECPAD plays a pivotal role in the cultural and remembrance policy, via its exceptional archives that encompass 12 million photographs and 31,000 films. These archives are preserved and publicized through the sale of still images and movies; film and documentary productions; exhibitions; and books. Finally, the ECPAD also provides training in audiovisual techniques.

ecpa ▶ d

AGENCE D'IMAGES
DE LA DÉFENSE

Acknowledgments

The publisher would like to thank the French Ministry of Defense and its heritage departments for the trust they have placed in us for several years:

– at the DMPA: Myriam Achari, head of the Directorate of Remembrance, Heritage and Archives; Alexis Neviaski, head of the Cultural Heritage unit; Mathilde Meyer, director of publications within the Cultural Heritage unit.

– at the ECPAD: Christophe Jacquot, director; Gilles Ciment, assistant director; Charlotte Taisne de Mullet, head of communications; Xavier Sené, head of conservation unit and promotion of archives (PCVA); Gabrielle Touret, assistant to the head of the conservation unit and promotion of archives (PCVA) responsible for promotion; Alexandra Berdeaux, head of the department of image sales (DVI); Vincent Blondeau, head of CVI clientele; Nathalie Sarvac, head of the conservation and archival department (DCS); Yann Prieux of the DCS photographic technical unit; Emmanuel Thomassin, head of the department of documentary additions (DED) of the PCVA.

The author and publisher would like to extend special thanks to Albane Brunel and Véronique Goloubinoff, documentalists responsible for the "World War I" collection at the ECPAD, the former for her enthusiastic involvement in selecting the photographs and the latter for the captions.

The author would like to thank his editor Anne Lemaire and the staff at Gallimard for their superb editorial work, Lisa Davidson and Elizabeth Ayre, for the English translation, Stéphane Audoin-Rouzeau, Jennifer D. Keene, and also Mattie Fitch, Cameron Givens, and Christian Gray.

MINISTRY OF DEFENSE

Jean-Yves Le Drian, Minister of Defense
Cédric Lewandowski, Chief of staff
Hubert Tardy-Joubert, Cultural advisor
Jean-Paul Bodin, Administrative secretary general
Myriam Achari, head of the Directorate of Remembrance, Heritage, and Archives

ÉDITIONS GALLIMARD

Department of illustrated books: Nathalie Bailleux
Series editor: Anne Lemaire
Art director: Anne Lagarrigue
Graphic design: Samuel Avequin
Layout: Virginie Lafon
Translation: Lisa Davidson and Elizabeth Ayre
Partnerships: Manuèle Destors
Production: Marie-Agnès Naturel

Photoengraving: Reproscan, Italy
Printed in Italy by Graphicom